JEREMIAH
Man and Prophet

JEREMIAH
Man and Prophet

SHELDON H. BLANK

Hebrew Union College–Jewish Institute of Religion

HEBREW UNION COLLEGE PRESS
Cincinnati   1961

For information, write University Publishers Inc.
239 Park Avenue South, New York 3, N. Y.

FIRST EDITION

Library of Congress Catalog Card Number: 61-14333

Manufactured in the United States of America
by Quinn & Boden Company, Inc., Rahway, N. J.

For

MIMS AND MURRAY, BITS AND JOE
AND FOR THEIR GENERATIONS

Foreword

This book is a publication of the Alumni Association of the Hebrew Union College—Jewish Institute of Religion. A quinquennial fund, to which its members contribute, is set aside for the specific purpose of encouraging its members to pursue studies in Judaism with the prospect of publication, and it is also used to publish manuscripts of the Faculty of our Alma Mater. Among these publications are the volumes by Dr. Kaufmann Kohler, Dr. David Neumark, Dr. Jacob Z. Lauterbach, Dr. Samuel Sandmel, and Dr. Solomon B. Freehof.

As in every instance, the views of the author do not necessarily represent those of the members of the Association. We select a manuscript as representing sound scholarship and a contribution to the general understanding of an important subject.

Dr. Sheldon Blank is an alumnus of the Hebrew Union College, ordained a Rabbi in 1923. Following his undergraduate studies at the University of Cincinnati (B.A., M.A.), he continued his studies at the University of Jena (Ph.D.), Cambridge University, Hebrew University and American School of Oriental Research at Jerusalem. He

has been Professor of Bible at the Hebrew Union College
—Jewish Institute of Religion since 1926. He is a member
of many scholarly societies, and has served some of them
as President. His writings include "The Confessions of
✓Jeremiah and the Meaning of Prayer," "The Mission of
Israel—Biblical Origins," "Men Against God—The Pro-
methean Element in Biblical Prayer," and *Prophetic Faith
in Isaiah.*

Preface

In my *Prophetic Faith in Isaiah* (New York and London, 1958) I undertook to analyze a biblical book. Here I attempt to understand a biblical prophet; I set out to discover a person.

Earlier studies prepared the way for the middle chapters of this work. Chapters VIII to XI draw upon essays of mine which appeared in the *Hebrew Union College Annual:* "The Confessions of Jeremiah and the Meaning of Prayer" and " 'Doest Thou Well to be Angry?' A Study in Self-Pity" (*HUCA*, XXI-1948 and XXVI-1955) and, as *The Goldenson Lecture for 1955, "Of a Truth the Lord Hath Sent Me" An Inquiry into the Source of the Prophet's Authority* (H.U.C. Press, Cincinnati, 1955).

The translations from the Hebrew Bible are my own unless they are otherwise marked. They are sometimes paraphrastic. Square brackets enclose words which I supply for clarity, and a row of three dots replaces a word or words which I omit either because a condensed quotation serves my purpose sufficiently or, occasionally, because in their present textual form or context the omitted words yield no plausible sense.

ix

I owe much to my revered teacher Moses Buttenwieser and his thoughtful book *The Prophets of Israel* (Macmillan, 1914). I have made much use of the excellent commentary by Paul Volz: *Der Prophet Jeremia* (vol. X of the Sellin *Kommentar z.AT*, Leipzig, 1928). Though I highly esteem the works of John Skinner (*Prophecy and Religion*, Cambridge, 1922) and Adam C. Welch (*Jeremiah: His Times and His Work*, Oxford, 1928), I am not aware that either of these writings has directly influenced my thinking.

My students have doubtless done quite as much for me as my teachers, and I am endlessly grateful to them for unintended as well as for conscious help. To Amy Blank, my wife, to two of my colleagues, Provost Samuel Sandmel and Professor Eugene Mihaly, and to a former colleague, Dr. Hillel Fine, I owe a special word of thanks for their careful reading of my manuscript. Although I would not hold them accountable for any of the shortcomings of this book, I can truly say that their comments led me to clarify a number of obscurities and to think out more than a few half-thought conclusions. For her friendly help with the indexes I am very grateful to Mrs. Fanny Berg.

To my good friend of many years, Herman E. Snyder, President of the Alumni Association of the Hebrew Union College–Jewish Institute of Religion, to David Polish, Chairman of the Publications Committee of the Association—a substantial number of whom studied Jeremiah along with me and by refusing to be too easily satisfied helped me to write this book—I express my warm appreciation because they now are sponsoring its publication.

S. H. B.

Cincinnati, January 1961

Contents

Section III

WHAT JEREMIAH SAID

JEREMIAH
Man and Prophet

Introduction

No prophet sits for his portrait so well as the Prophet
Jeremiah. There is a full record of his life and thought.
The biblical book which contains his story—in the section
of the Bible called "The Prophets"—is one of the three
longer books there. It comes between the books of Isaiah
and Ezekiel and its size entitles Jeremiah to be known,
like them, as a "major" prophet.

Jeremiah is a good subject for a portrait not only because of the length of the record, but also because of
an unusual feature in the story: the prophet here sometimes speaks of himself. A biblical prophet rarely speaks
of himself—autobiographically—but Jeremiah does so; and
when he does he is more articulate than others. He is
co-operative, and from the sources a plausible portrait
looks out.

Historically, Jeremiah is to be associated with the fall
of Jerusalem in 587 B.C. and the beginning of the Babylonian Exile. He was not the first of the writing prophets.
About a hundred years before his time a great cluster of
such prophets addressed themselves to the people of
Israel. They are well known; Amos and Hosea, Micah

3

and Isaiah were among them. Their time was roughly from 750 to 700 B.C., the latter half of the eighth pre-Christian century, and we often refer to them as "the eighth-century prophets." Jeremiah learned a great deal from them.

It was in the following century, the seventh, that Jeremiah appeared. The five decades between 630 and 580 B.C. include the years of his activity. Ezekiel was a younger contemporary of his, active at the beginning of the sixth century. The two of them, Jeremiah and Ezekiel, served as prophetic interpreters of a major crisis in Jewish history. They saw and experienced and interpreted the fall of Jerusalem and the beginning of the Babylonian captivity. Jeremiah was intimately involved in those events.

The relatively peaceful years of his activity were the time of Assyria's decline. Jeremiah saw the great Assyrian empire fold before the rising power of Babylonia. He saw too that Judah lay in Babylonia's path. He was there later when Nebuchadrezzar the Babylonian took Jerusalem, destroyed the city with its proud temple, exiled masses of the Judean populace and, for a while at least, put an end to the little kingdom of Judah. When treachery further reduced the small remnant of a state entrusted to the Jewish provincial governor Gedaliah, Jeremiah was still among the people. He went unwillingly with a fugitive group of them to Egypt. No doubt he died in Egypt soon after the climactic disasters of those last years.

A prophet deserves honor not because he foresees the coming event but because he sees the meaning within the current event. It is the prophet's gift of insight, not his foresight, that sets him apart. Although Amos rightly foresaw the Assyrian conquest of the Northern Kingdom in 722 B.C. and although Jeremiah correctly foresaw the Babylonian conquest of the Southern Kingdom in 587 B.C., neither prophet's honor derives from the accuracy of his political predictions. It derives from his pained recognition of the fundamental causes making for his nation's impending collapse. The prophet saw a pattern in human society (he called it God), according to which pattern a rotting social structure, like a condemned building, must collapse. An Amos, or later a Jeremiah, saw fatal decay in his own society and experienced concern. (An active concern always impregnates a prophet's insight.) So he sounded the alarm. Like Amos and the others, Jeremiah sounded frantic warnings, not in anger but in pain, and appealed for measures designed to buttress the tottering structure. What he was given to see and what he was moved to do for his people made Jeremiah a prophet.

Through turbulent times Jeremiah lived a turbulent life. The two sources which his book contains conspire to reveal the tumult of his life and the conflict in his heart. Section I of the present work draws on the first of these sources. This is the longer source. It is a biographer's *third person narrative*, a sympathetic eyewitness account of certain dramatic events in the life of the prophet. The second source is the remarkable series of autobiographical notes, the *documents of self-revelation*, scattered through the columns of Jeremiah's book. These documents provide an emotional accompaniment to the more factual biographical narrative. They are what make the portrait possible. But the analysis of these latter documents is often difficult and they are better understood with the biographical account as background. For that reason they are reserved for study in Section II.

An analysis of these combined sources yields a view

of a sensitive prophet's religious experience. It provides an example of the personal religion of biblical man. It even throws some light on the meaning of revelation.

Section III deals more particularly with the content of Jeremiah's message. It looks more narrowly at the prophetic word. It asks *what Jeremiah said,* what values he disclosed. It is concerned with values.

Jeremiah was one of those prophets who saw no security except in justice and believed that the only safe society was the just society. Dismayed by what he saw about him Jeremiah went with grim tidings reluctantly to his people to warn and exhort them. To his peril he sought them out even in the precincts of the Jerusalem temple. He spoke of his people's ruin as an Amos had done before him, and a Micah, an Isaiah and others—but Jeremiah spoke also of their eventual restoration. He hoped that Jerusalem would be rebuilt, although he was convinced that destruction was the city's immediate fate. He knew—we will yet ask how he knew—that his people must be uprooted—would be replanted. This hope of his—this hope beyond despair—is a particular feature of Jeremiah's message, a new shape, a contribution which he makes to the unfolding prophetic vision. It is among the values which Jeremiah disclosed.

But Jeremiah's foremost contribution is his perspective. Jeremiah's insight led him to a vastly deepened perspective. That perspective is a lastingly significant value.

Section *I*

The Life of a Prophet

I

On Trial for Treason

The biographer's narrative does not start with Jeremiah's childhood and youth, nor even with the beginning of his career as prophet. The earliest dated event recorded in the narrative source is Jeremiah's "temple sermon" with its immediate drastic consequences, the threat to Jeremiah's life, his trial for treason. Jeremiah stood trial because he spoke a dread word which came to him from God "early in the reign of Jehoiakim, Josiah's son, king of Judah" (26:1)—that is to say about the year 609 B.C. Jeremiah would then have been perhaps forty years of age, and this would be about twenty years after the probable beginning of his prophetic ministry.[1] The word which Jeremiah spoke early in the reign of Jehoiakim is to be found in his seventh chapter.

This is the utterance which called down the wrath of the people upon the head of the prophet Jeremiah:

> Hear God's word, all Judah who enter these gates to worship God. Thus said the Lord of hosts, the God of Israel:

[1] The reader who has interest for more historical detail and who wishes to follow the analysis with open Bible will find help in the First Additional Note on pp. 232 ff., which includes a table of the kings in Jeremiah's life and a table of chapters in order of treatment here in Section I.

9

Improve your ways and your doings and I will allow you to dwell in this place. Do not rely on delusions and say: "The temple of God, the temple of God, the temple of God are these." For only if you improve your ways and your doings—only if you promote justice between man and man, do not oppress stranger, orphan or widow . . . and do not go after other gods to your hurt, only then will I allow you to dwell in this place (in the land which I gave to your fathers) forever and ever. Lo, you rely on profitless delusions. Will you steal, kill, engage in adultery, swear to falsehood, sacrifice to Baal and go after other gods whom you knew not and come and stand before me in this house . . . and say: "We are safe"? . . . Does this house . . . seem to you to be a bandit's cave? So do I regard it, God says.

Just go to my place which was at Shiloh . . . and observe what I did to it because of the wickedness of my people Israel. Now then, God says, because you did these things, and because though I spoke to you earnestly you did not listen, and because you did not respond when I called you, I will do to this house . . . on which you rely, and to the place which I gave to you and your fathers, what I did to Shiloh, and I will cast you off as I cast off your brothers, all the spawn of Ephraim (7:1-15).

What especially Jeremiah said in the "temple sermon" was this: that God would destroy the Jerusalem temple, doing now to it what in an earlier generation he "did to Shiloh." The prophet's reference to Shiloh was ominous. Shiloh had been a sanctuary city like Jerusalem, but the Philistines had destroyed it long before,[2] and the occur- miah's day, the men of Jerusalem "in the gate of God's rence was a bitter historical recollection. Now in Jere-

[2] These are the implications of I Sam. 1-6; note that when the ark was recovered it was not returned to Shiloh (I Sam. 7:1).

house" heard the incredible word that God both could and would assign this latter "house" to ruin, the consequence of his people's misconduct, history repeating itself. They heard the proclamation with disbelief and consternation, for they thought of the temple as the very source and symbol of their security. But they heard it also with dread and anger, because words had effective reality and it was dangerous to say such things. Even a prophet of the stature of Jeremiah could not say such things with impunity.

If one is to understand the consequences for Jeremiah of that "temple sermon" one has first to sense the shock that it imparted. The centuries have tamed the words and we read them in armchair ease; sentiments repeated for twenty-five hundred years may lose their edge. But were it possible for us to hear Jeremiah's words as though for the first time, and to hear them with the whole substructure of confidence that supported Jeremiah's first audience, we too would recoil in amazed horror. When he spoke them they were wild—sounds that make men shrink and cringe, that make them put their fingers in their ears and grin embarrassed, that prompt them to say Piffle! and Nonsense! and to jeer for comfort, or compel them to prosecute the crackpot with his crazy talk. Jeremiah might well have expected such treatment as he in fact received.

Possibly, place and time had something to do with the violence of the popular reaction to his words.

God sent Jeremiah to the gate of the Jerusalem temple to deliver his message, and the place was right: the people's reliance on the Jerusalem temple was the target of his words. And the time was right; the people of all Judah were converging on the religious capital of their land to discharge what they supposed to be their periodic cultic obligation, to celebrate a pilgrimage festival with sacrifice as was their custom. The place and time were right enough, but also they were among the ingredients that gave the situation its explosive quality. For Jeremiah went to that one place at just that time to say that what the throng was bent on doing there was worse than futile, was indeed offensive to the God whom they were hoping thus to please. What he went there to say was designed to slip the foundations out from under the structure of their traditional faith. Jeremiah asked for something different, something better than the religion they knew: "Improve your ways and your doings," he said. What they were about was not enough, was not good. The prophet called reliance on the temple a false confidence. With a sweeping gesture he damned the whole cult complex: "Do not rely on delusions and say: 'The temple of God, the temple of God, the temple of God are these.'"

From where he stood his one gesture could embrace all the buildings and the throng. Place, time, and message combined to make the occurrence an occasion.

In what he said Jeremiah stood with Amos, who had proclaimed in God's name:

I hate, I reject your festival offerings,
I have no pleasure in your assembly sacrifices
(Amos 5:21).

He took his place also with Isaiah who had said for God:

. . . I am sated with offerings of rams
And fat of fed beasts . . .
Who asked this of you—
To trample my courts? . . .
Your new moons and holy days
I hate . . . (Isa. 1:11, 12, 14).

Still with Amos and with Isaiah, Jeremiah knew the other way, the way acceptable to God. As against the wrong way Amos before him had proposed:

> But let justice roll as waters   *Am*
> And righteousness as a steady stream (5:24).

And Isaiah had phrased the same demand in his incisive imperatives:

> Cease doing wrong, learn to do good.
> Seek justice. Correct oppression.
> Secure the orphan's right.
> Take up the widow's cause (1:16 f.).

This was the prophetic tradition which claimed Jeremiah. Speaking a hundred years or more after Amos and Isaiah, Jeremiah rephrased and paired the same divine warning and demand, saying:

> Only if you promote justice between man and man, do not oppress stranger, orphan or widow . . . and do not go after other gods to your hurt, only then will I allow you to dwell in this place.

To reject the right way and to adopt the wrong way were equally disastrous, he said:

> Lo, you rely on profitless delusions. Will you steal, kill, engage in adultery, swear to falsehood, sacrifice to Baal . . . and come and stand before me in this house . . . and say: "We are safe"?

Unquestionably Jeremiah stood in the prophetic succession.

Not this alone—he cultivated another tradition as well.

He knew of "the ten commandments." When he asked:
"Will you steal, kill, engage in adultery, swear to falsehood . . . go after other gods . . . ?" in effect he was
asking: How many of the "ten commandments" would you
defy—and with presumed impunity? The deuteronomic
version of the Decalogue, probably shaped only a little
while before Jeremiah went to speak in the temple, sounds
through his challenge:

> You shall have no other gods before me . . .
> You shall not kill.
> You shall not engage in adultery.
> You shall not steal.
> You shall not bear false witness against
>   one another (Deut. 5:7, 17-20).

However ancient or recent this "Mosaic" tradition may
be, there is an obvious affinity between the Decalogue
and the Jeremianic formula for survival. And if in the
days of Jeremiah tablets inscribed with this Decalogue
were enclosed in the ark within the holy of holies, then
this was one feature of the temple which Jeremiah did
not wholly reject. There is, however, a significant difference between the prophet's demands and the formulation
in the Decalogue. Whereas the Decalogue lists first the
duties to God, Jeremiah's list commences with man's
behavior towards man: "Will you steal, kill, engage in
adultery, swear to falsehood . . . ?" and only then goes
on with "sacrifice to Baal . . . go after other gods . . . ?"
Nevertheless, being in part so like the Decalogue, in part
so like the words of an Amos or an Isaiah, Jeremiah's
words could not have shocked his hearers by reason of
their novelty alone.

With Isaiah and with Micah, Jeremiah shared even his basic heresy. Isaiah had said: "The Lord of hosts will come down to lay siege to Zion and her hill" (Isa. 31:4) and Micah had said much the same, as will yet appear. What Jeremiah said was that the inhabitants of Judah, consuming one another in their greed, had forfeited all security. Because of their false dealings, they were now no longer safe—even here in the shadow of the sanctuary. The temple in their midst was no guarantee at all; the temple itself was doomed. Of all that Jeremiah said, this is what the people heard. This is what his accusers picked up and cited against him in court when they asked the death sentence. "A death sentence for the man, because he prophesied against this city, as you plainly heard!"—What the people "plainly heard" was the threat which ends the address in chapter 7, the sermon delivered at the temple gate, the words: "I will do to this house . . . what I did to Shiloh, and I will cast you off as I cast off your brothers, all the spawn of Ephraim."

In essentially the same form the biographical account in chapter 26 resumes these concluding words—resumes and repeats them—does so twice, because clearly they were the provocation. This, now, is the story of the trial:

Early in the reign of Jehoiakim, Josiah's son, king of Judah, this word came from God:
So God said: Stand in the court of God's house and speak to all the cities of Judah who come to worship in God's house all of the words which I have charged you to speak to them; omit no word. Perhaps they will listen and turn each from his evil way and I will relent concerning the evil which I have prepared for them because of the evil of their doings. And you shall say to them: So God has said: If you do not listen to me . . . then I will treat this house like

Shiloh and will make this city for all the nations of the
earth a byword to be used in a curse.

Now the priests and the prophets . . . heard Jeremiah
speak these words in God's house and when Jeremiah had
finished speaking all that God had charged him to speak
to the whole people, then the priests and the prophets . . .
seized him, saying: "You must die. Why did you prophesy
in God's name: This house will be like Shiloh and this city
ruined and uninhabited?" So the whole people assembled
against Jeremiah in God's house. And the princes of Judah
heard of these matters and went up from the king's house
to God's house and held session at the entrance of the new
gate of God['s house]. And the priests and the prophets
said to the princes and the whole people: "A death sentence
for this man, because he prophesied against this city, as
you plainly heard!" (26:1-11).

Ch.26

That then was the provocation, that he prophesied:
"This house will be like Shiloh and this city ruined and
uninhabited"—that he spoke these thoughts at the very
gate of the temple in the ears of a worshipful gathering,
confident by reason of their piety. That was the statement
that the accused Jeremiah had either to withdraw or to
defend.

Jeremiah pleaded guilty; he said that indeed he had
spoken thus on God's behalf.

Then Jeremiah said to all the princes and the whole people:
"It was God who sent me to prophesy against this house
and against this city all of the words which you have heard.
So now improve your ways and your doings and listen to
the voice of the Lord your God and he will relent concerning the evil which he spoke over them. As for me, I am in
your hands; do to me as is right and pleasing to you. Yet,
you must know that if you kill me you take on yourselves,

on the city, and on its inhabitants the guilt of [spilling] innocent blood, for truly God sent me to speak to you all of these words" (26:12-15).

Jeremiah's defense plea contributed no new substantive evidence. His accusers had asked: "Why did you prophesy in God's name: This house will be like Shiloh and this city ruined and uninhabited?" And he answered confirming the terms of the question: "It was God who sent me to prophesy against this house and against this city all of the words which you have heard." And again: "Truly, God sent me to speak to you all of these words." In effect he said: "You heard me aright. I did indeed say it. I said it indeed in God's name."

Jeremiah did not add as he might have done (since it is the longer statement in his seventh chapter that is under attack): "You overlooked my appeal to you, which was as much a part of God's word as the threat that went with it." He did not say: "You overlooked it" but he did repeat his appeal, and he repeated the conditional promise: "So now improve your ways and your doings and listen to the voice of the Lord your God and he will relent concerning the evil. . . ."

His accusers may have been demanding that he roundly deny his position, recall his threats and void them. Their safety may have seemed to demand that he revoke, annul, neutralize, reverse, or check the leaven which he had planted in the form of damning words. But if so, Jeremiah had to disappoint them. He could only say his words over again—for those were the words—and propose that his people must do what was to be done. It was not for him to recant, for he truly said what God sent him to say; it was for them to act. You must first "improve your ways

and your doings . . ." he said, and then God "will relent
concerning the evil which he spoke." The prophet has
spoken and he will not—can not—call back his words.

What recourse then do the people have? A very few
years later Jeremiah's words will be put down in ink on
a scroll, and to rid himself of the dangers lurking in the
writing a king will slash and burn the scroll, destroy it
to remove its baneful influence. But what possible recourse
is there against the spoken word, once it is uttered by
a determined man?

Frustrated in their attempt to induce Jeremiah to recall and annul his spoken words, of necessity the prophet's
accusers require his life. The logic of their faith in the
power, for good or evil, inherent in the spoken word made
Jeremiah's death a needful consequence of his obstinacy.
If he would not provide the antidote, then they must find
one. They must obliterate the impudent speaker of doom
—must do so as a national security measure.

Jeremiah doubtless knew their logic, understood that
his defense was an exasperation and no satisfaction to
them, understood their asking the death sentence. Therefore his perplexity and his surrender: "As for me I am in
your hands; do to me as is right and pleasing to you.
[Here, too, he said nothing of which the court was not
already aware. Of course he was in their hands. With or
without his permission they would do with him as they
pleased.] Yet, you must know that if you kill me you take
on yourselves, on the city, and on its inhabitants the guilt
of [spilling] innocent blood, for truly God sent me to
speak to you all of these words."

If he brought any argument in defense of himself, he
did so in this final sentence. For, what he may here be
saying is this: "You fail of your purpose. You do not by

removing me eliminate the author of the words which you have heard, the words which you fear."

Two factors suggest the conclusion that this was indeed his argument. The one is a syntactical feature of Jeremiah's plea, and the other is the logic of the verdict. As for the former, the position of the word "truly" in the Hebrew sentence lends it emphasis: *"truly God sent me. . . ."* At the end and at the beginning of his plea Jeremiah underlined this point. For, at the beginning also, the order of the words makes for emphasis: "[It was not my own doing, nor did another man send me.] *It was God* who sent me to prophesy . . . all of the words which you have heard." So, it is a point which he is making. "It was God . . . truly."

As for the logic of the verdict, the judges found for Jeremiah, decided in his favor, and explained their decision:

> Then the princes and the whole people said to the priests and the prophets: "No death sentence for this man, inasmuch as he has spoken to us in the name of the Lord our God" (26:16).

In view of the accusation which opened the trial the verdict as explained is somewhat unexpected. Was it not already granted that Jeremiah spoke "in God's name"? When the priests and the prophets seized him they said: "You must die" and they asked: "Why did you prophesy in God's name: This house will be like Shiloh and this city ruined and uninhabited?" And yet it was just because he spoke "in the name of the Lord" that the court let him off. So it would seem indeed that he had made a point of this speaking in God's name.

It would seem also that he had managed to put some new meaning into the phrase. When his accusers first asked why he thus spoke in God's name they meant less than his judges meant when at the end they released him because he had, as he claimed, in fact spoken in God's name. Possibly, his plea brought to life the disturbing awareness that not the prophet but God was the veritable source and author of the looming threat—and that removing God's prophet would accomplish nothing material.

But the fact remains that Jeremiah produced no substantive evidence in his own defense. He only made statements. And this is significant. It is significant that the prophet (perhaps the most articulate prophet of all), when hardest pressed, fighting indeed for his life, could do no more than state: "It was God who sent me . . . truly God sent me." Apparently there was no more to say—or at any rate nothing better to say. And his acquittal means that Jeremiah handled his defense with skill and judgment, however unconvincing at this distance his argument may sound.

Or was it his defense plea alone which saved his life? The reason which the court coupled with its verdict does indeed suggest that it was his own argument which won him his case—and that is why this reason stands where it does. However, it is not to be denied that another argument lays claim to some of the credit for his acquittal —the argument from the precedent of Micah the Morashtite. The precedent of Micah is invoked in a paragraph of the report which now follows on the verdict acquitting Jeremiah. The biographer appears not to have described the progress of the trial step by step in temporal sequence, because it can hardly be doubted that the elders arose to quote the precedent at some point before the court rendered the verdict, if not indeed before Jeremiah spoke on his own behalf. Logically the verb which begins the Micah paragraph must be a pluperfect: "Now men *had* arisen. . . ."

> Now men had arisen of the elders of the land and said to the whole assembly of the people: "Micah the Morashtite prophesied in the time of Hezekiah, king of Judah, and said to all of the people of Judah: 'So the God of hosts has said: Zion will be ploughed up as a field, Jerusalem will be ruins and the hill of the House a forested height.' Did Hezekiah, king of Judah, or all Judah think of putting him to death? Did he [Hezekiah] not fear God and supplicate God so that God relented concerning the evil which he spoke over them? But we are bent on doing ourselves great harm" (26:17-19).

The concluding clause is proof that this defense of Jeremiah, which certain elders undertook, was entered before the court released him. "We are bent on doing ourselves great harm" has meaning only if spoken while it still appeared that Jeremiah would be put to death.[3]

At whatever point in the trial it was cited, the precedent of Micah was relevant, and it may well have influenced the court. This is unique in prophetic literature. Nowhere else is one of the literary prophets quoted by name in the book of another. This Micah the Morashtite was among the Twelve, one who gave his name to a book. The elders have quoted accurately from the end of his third chapter:

---

[3] I am indebted to my teacher Moses Buttenwieser for the translation "we are bent on doing"; see his *The Prophets of Israel* (New York, 1914), p. 26, and in general his treatment of "the temple-sermon" there (pp. 21-51).

Therefore, because of you
Zion will be ploughed up as a field,
Jerusalem will be ruins
And the hill of the House will be forested heights
(Mic. 3:12).

The elders have a long memory. Micah's words moved
King Hezekiah to prayer more than a hundred years before the trial of Jeremiah. Whether through oral trans-
mission or already in written form, the words of Micah
had remained alive during that century and were at hand
for the elders to quote. The elders even had a tradition
which Micah's book does not preserve, the tradition that
Micah not only escaped ill treatment but even experienced
some success with Hezekiah, who feared and supplicated
God "so that God relented concerning the evil which he
spoke over them." There is of course a comparable tradition about Hezekiah in the legendary chapters 36 and 37
of Isaiah. By his pious demeanor there, the king obtained a
reprieve and the Assyrian withdrawal. We can no longer
determine whether this tradition attached itself first to
Isaiah (in which event the elders confuse Isaiah with his
contemporary, Micah) or whether the tradition first belonged to Micah only to be adopted subsequently by the
author of the Isaiah legends. The latter may seem the
more probable in view of the elders' accuracy when they
cited the words of Micah.

Incidentally, they could have cited words of Isaiah
as well, because he too pronounced the doom of Jerusalem,
and did so unmolested:

As the lion growls,
The young lion over its prey,
[And] though there be assembled against him

A full band of shepherds
He fears not their shouting
And is not disturbed by their tumult,
Just so the Lord of hosts will come down
To lay siege to Zion and her hill (Isa. 31:4).

It was obviously less hazardous to speak thus of Jerusalem at the end of the eighth century, in the days of Micah, Isaiah, Hezekiah, and Assyria than it was at the end of the seventh, in the days of Jeremiah, Jehoiakim, and Babylonia—and the days of Uriah the prophet.

The report of Jeremiah's trial acquired an appendix. This concerns another prophet, Uriah of Kiriath Yearim, who prophesied "words much like those of Jeremiah" still in the days of Jekoiakim and who, unlike Jeremiah, did not escape the tragic consequences. The form of this latter narrative indeed suggests that it is an appendix, not, like the previous paragraph, a precedent cited at Jeremiah's trial. If Uriah had spoken before Jeremiah, the narrator would hardly say he prophesied "words much like those of Jeremiah." The Uriah case followed on Jeremiah's acquittal and for our understanding should begin with the word "Subsequently."

[Subsequently] another man, Uriah, Shcmaiah's son, of Kiriath Yearim, prophesied in God's name, and prophesied of this city and of this land words much like those of Jeremiah. And the king Jehoiakim and all his warriors and all the princes feared his words and the king undertook to kill him. Uriah heard and fled and came to Egypt, but the king Jehoiakim sent . . . Elnathan, Akbor's son, and men with him to Egypt and they fetched Uriah away from Egypt and brought him to the king Jehoiakim, and he put him to the sword and cast his body on the people's graves.

Ahikam, Shafan's son, had, however, intervened for
Jeremiah, so that he was not given over to the people
for death (26:20-24).

What the supplement adds to the report of Jeremiah's
trial is, on the one hand, the name of Ahikam, a partisan
of Jeremiah, possibly one of the elders who quoted the
Micah precedent in his favor, and the name of a prophet
who shared Jeremiah's conviction that Jerusalem was
doomed—evidence that Jeremiah in his day was not fighting a lone battle, and, on the other hand, grim proof in
retrospect that Jeremiah escaped execution by a hair's
breadth.

But he did escape. And this fact is impressive. He stood
his ground defenseless, saying only that he knew, and
his assuredness won the day. The people allowed him to
say unharmed what with such certainty he knew. For the
present he still might go about his business of speaking.

II

A King Burns Jeremiah's Book

F our years later they burned Jeremiah's "book." The story is told in his thirty-sixth chapter. First he wrote the book:

> In the fourth year of Jehoiakim, Josiah's son, king of Judah, Jeremiah had this word from God: Take you a book roll and write in it all that I have said to you about Jerusalem and Judah . . . from the time when I spoke to you in the days of Josiah until now (36:1 f.).

cl 3 6

The "book" could have been fairly large; twenty-three years had passed since Jeremiah became God's prophet. In this passage here dated in Jehoiakim's fourth year, that is 606, Jeremiah says: "I have had the word of God since Josiah's thirteenth year [638] . . . now for twenty-three years" (25:3).[1] What he had said in these twenty-three years was now to be written down for another attempt at communication. "Perhaps," God says. It is an important word—'ulai, perhaps . . . , on the chance that . . . , because it is yet possible. . . .

[1] Compare 1:2.

25

Perhaps the house of Judah will give heed to the harm which I propose to do them and so turn each from his evil way that I may pardon their guilt and their sin (36:3).

It is purposive—God's use of Jeremiah; he wants to be enabled to pardon. Not here alone, again and again the prophetic message is phrased as an appeal. "Improve your ways and your doings," four years earlier Jeremiah had urged upon his people, then also on the chance, *'ulai,* and had barely escaped a death sentence for his pains.[2] So now he was to make a record of the recurrent appeals which had been the constant theme of his activity "since Josiah's thirteenth year." For thus Jeremiah summed up his labor in a phrase:

> I have had the word of God . . . now for twenty-three years . . . and have earnestly said to you . . . : "Return each of you from his wicked way and from the evil of his doings and so abide in the land which God gave you . . ." (25:3, 5).

He reduced his labor to a formula, to an epigram lost in translation: *shuvu . . . u-shevu,* "return . . . and abide." The combination of imperatives produces a conditional sentence. It means: If you return you may abide in the land. But the imperative forms express yet more of the prophet's meaning; they express his desire. He would urge, plead, command if he could, the people's return, so that pardon might follow. It was with such purpose that he went about the recording of his message.

> Jeremiah called Baruch, Neriyah's son, and Baruch wrote in a book roll at Jeremiah's dictation all of the words which God had spoken to him (36:4).

[2] Compare 7:3; 26:3.

Then, after they had written the book, Jeremiah and Baruch awaited an opportunity. When the people of Judah assembled again at Jerusalem, this time because the king had proclaimed a fast, they acted. Jeremiah charged Baruch to take with him the book and to go to God's house; Jeremiah sent Baruch to read the book publicly to all who congregated there from the cities of Judah,[3] for Jeremiah thought:

> Perhaps (*'ulai*) their supplication will fall before God and they will return each from his evil way, for great is the anger and the wrath with which God has threatened his people (36:7).

And Baruch did as he was told.

A phrase in the narrative reveals why Baruch and not Jeremiah went to deliver God's word. "I am *'azur*," Jeremiah says; "I can not go to God's house" (v. 5), and he means "I am in hiding." In I Chron. 12:1 the word *'azur* occurs with this meaning: "These are they who joined David at Ziklag while he was hiding (*'azur*) from Saul."[4] But if he had been acquitted why should Jeremiah have been a fugitive? Two answers suggest themselves. Possibly he gave offense to the king and princes on a second occasion, one of which there is no record. Or else, perhaps despite his acquittal Jeremiah was not completely absolved of the old charge.[5] At any rate, Baruch appeared with Jeremiah's "book" because Jeremiah was keeping to himself—he was "prevented."

[3] The situation is clearer if 36:9 is read before 36:5.
[4] Compare I Sam. 23:19.
[5] Jehoiakim's subsequent execution of Uriah (see above, pp. 23 f.) could well have suggested to Jeremiah that he go underground. See also Buttenwieser, *The Prophets of Israel*, pp. 40-41.

Baruch read the book in public on the day of the national fast, and the unwished expected happened. Rather than take steps to remove conditions which called forth the threat, the government sought to remove the articulated threat and to close the mouth that spoke it. An officer heard the reading and reported it to the princes assembled at the palace. The princes to verify the report sent deputies, who brought in Baruch with the book roll, and they sat him down to read it to them. "And when they heard all the words," the narrative relates, "they were terrified and they said to each other: 'We have to tell these things to the king.'" But first they established responsibility. "Tell us," they said, "how you came to write these things. . . ." And Baruch told them: "He dictated all the words to me aloud and I wrote them with ink in the book." In this matter they dealt fairly enough. Even as the court had released Jeremiah when it appeared that not he but God was the source of his prophecies, so in this analogous situation the princes dismissed Baruch. "Go," they said. "Hide yourself with Jeremiah." But they sequestered the book and they told the king (36:10-20). He took prompt action:

> Then the king sent Yehudi to fetch the scroll from the chamber of the scribe Elishama, and Yehudi read it aloud before the king and the attendant princes, while in that ninth month the king was seated in his winter house with fire in a burner before him. And as Yehudi read three or four columns he slashed it with a pen knife and threw it on the fire in the burner until the whole scroll was consumed (36:21-23).

Why the king and his court proceeded methodically to destroy the book becomes clear as the account unfolds.

When first the princes had heard the words read they had been thrown into consternation—they were "terrified" (*pahadu*) (v. 16). For Israel in the days of Jeremiah a spoken threat had substance and effective reality. A threat, for example, like that in 5:14 was not a poetic figure. If God said to Jeremiah,

> I will make fire of my words in your mouth
> And of this people fuel, and it will consume them,

the phrases were not taken for empty imagery. No, God's words through Jeremiah were fire and the menace was real. A written threat was equally terrifying—so long as the writing lasted. But once the scroll has been reduced to shreds and ashes the danger is over. After the biographer has told of the book's destruction he at once concludes this episode in the account with the bare statement:

> And the king and his servants who had heard the words were not terrified nor did they rend their garments (v. 24).

Of course not; the prophylactic knife and fire had given them back their confidence.

Nevertheless, the king now ordered the arrest of Baruch and Jeremiah. "But God kept them hidden," the narrator says, though the Greek translation has a more prosaic reading: ". . . they were in hiding" (v. 26).

What this narrative reveals of the life of Jeremiah is the fact that his acquittal four years previously, though good in its time, was really no more than an episode in a train of painful events in his long experience of pain. He had escaped the death penalty, but prudence soon suggested that he go into hiding—a living death for one whose role it is to speak. Under such circumstances a Baruch becomes a necessity. From his place of refuge Jeremiah sent forth this disciple with his written word. Lacking the prophet they let the disciple go free but they burned the message. They denied the prophet his essence by destroying his words—for what is a prophet if he does not communicate? —and again they threatened him. A warrant was out for the arrest of Jeremiah together with his scribe.

In some cave perhaps, like David and his men concealed from Saul, or like Elijah, a fugitive from the wrath of Jezebel,[6] they waited. And while they waited they followed the example of Moses, who made good the broken tablets, and they repaired the damage which the king had done.

> Jeremiah had a word from God after the king had burned the scroll with the words that Baruch had written at Jeremiah's mouth: Take another scroll and write on it the former words, those that were on the former scroll which Jehoiakim, king of Judah, burned. And say of Jehoiakim, king of Judah, so God said: You burned this scroll asking: "Why did you write on it: the king of Babylon will come and lay this land waste and remove from it man and beast?" Therefore God has said of Jehoiakim, king of Judah: No one of his shall sit on David's throne, and his own body shall be cast out to the heat of the day and the cold of the night and I shall put upon him and his seed and his servants their guilt and bring on all the people of Jerusalem and Judah the harm with which I threatened them unheeded.
> So Jeremiah gave Baruch, his scribe, another scroll and he wrote therein from Jeremiah's mouth all the words of the book which Jehoiakim, king of Judah, had burned.
> But many more such words were added (36:27-32).

In addition to the thirty-sixth chapter, which is the account of the burning and the restoration of Jeremiah's

6 I Kings 19:8-9, and compare I Kings 18:4.

book, two others are dated to the fourth year of Jehoiakim: chapters 25 and 45. The suggestion is plausible that
along with some quite different material the first of these,
chapter 25, contains the introduction to the second scroll
which Baruch wrote at the mouth of Jeremiah. The reference there (in v. 13) to "all my words which I spoke over
[the land], all that is written in this book"—the reference
to "this book" in the same fourth year of Jehoiakim—
makes it wholly probable that a part of chapter 25 is the
original introduction to the newly dictated scroll of Jeremianic prophecies.

This is the section, the early part of this chapter, where
Jeremiah put up the burden of his twenty-three years' ministry in the epigrammatic formula: *shuvu* . . . *u-shevu*,
"return . . . and abide." If the verse (v. 4) which precedes this epitome is not the addition of a different hand
it is at least a parenthetical aside. Jeremiah himself, not
"all his servants the prophets," [7] phrased God's appeal in
this fashion. "Now for twenty-three years . . . I have
earnestly said to you . . . : Return. . . ." But the divine
word through Jeremiah went unheeded. With blade and
fire the king had undertaken to nullify it and now he
sought the prophet, perhaps with similar intent. But the
word was not to be denied, and what Baruch wrote now
on Jeremiah's second scroll was unambiguous and shock-
ing and specific:

> I am about to take all the tribes of the north, God says, and
> my servant Nebuchadrezzar, king of Babylon, and bring
> them in against this land and its people . . . and I will
> destroy [the land and people] and make [the land] an eerie
> desolation and a ruin forever. And I will end for them

[7] There is good reason to believe that this expression came into use
later than Jeremiah's time; see Blank, *Prophetic Faith in Isaiah* (New
York: Harper, 1958), pp. 107-10.

Sound of merriment and rejoicing,
Voice of bridegroom and of bride,
Sound of mill, and light of lamp.

. . . And I will bring against the land all my words which
I spoke over it, all that is written in this book (25:9-13).

The threat of Babylon is looming, and Jeremiah will have
much more to say of it—and suffer for saying it.

The other chapter from that same year, the forty-fifth
chapter, is a small scene from the life of Jeremiah and
Baruch. It is in many ways a revealing chapter, more important than its brevity would suggest. It is entitled: "The
word which the prophet Jeremiah spoke to Baruch,
Neriyah's son, when he wrote these words in a book at
the mouth of Jeremiah in the fourth year of Jehoiakim,
Josiah's son, king of Judah" (v. 1), and the title verse
dates the incident. "The word which the prophet Jeremiah
spoke to Baruch" in that year of the writing of the book
was a word of comfort and encouragement. To this de-
voted disciple who had accepted Jeremiah's lot, the
prophet conveyed a small promise—God had said that
when others perished Baruch would survive: "I will bring
disaster down upon all flesh, God says, but I will give you
your life as reward wherever you go" (45:5b).

Certain aspects of this chapter (Baruch's self-pity,[8]
God's rewarding the singly deserving[9]) will be considered in other contexts below, but in the present context
the chapter is significant for what it tells of Jeremiah's
life. In the hurt eyes of his friend his own suffering is reflected. Jeremiah could equally well have uttered Baruch's
complaint:

[8] See Chapter X, below.
[9] See below, pp. 211, 222 f.

> Alas! and Woe! God has added misery to my pain;
> I am worn out with my sighing and find no respite (45:3).

As fugitives together they were sharing hardships, and what the one suffered the other endured also. Baruch's complaint adds color to the record of events in the life of Jeremiah. The lot of the fugitives was bitter—but their exile was not endless.

III

False Prophets, False Hopes

Without detailing how that could be, Jeremiah's biographer put him again among the people. Jeremiah was active and vocal by the beginning of the reign of Zedekiah, if not sooner. His encounter with Hananiah in the twenty-eighth chapter is plainly dated there (v. 1) in Zedekiah's fourth year. That would be the year 594, twelve years after Jehoiakim burned the prophet's book and ordered his arrest. But Jeremiah apparently moved about freely again still earlier in the days of that same king Jehoiakim. His experience with the Rechabites in chapter 35 is dated to the reign of Jehoiakim (v. 1). This would be near the end of Jehoiakim's reign, because already Nebuchadrezzar had come into the land, and Judeans from the countryside were fleeing to Jerusalem for safety (so v. 11), probably in 598—eight years after the book burning. There is even one undated incident which may have occurred still earlier, the one recorded in chapters 19 and 20.

It is not clear what changes made it safe for Jeremiah to appear again in public. Did such friends as he had— the elders who cited the precedent of Micah at his trial,

34

among them perhaps Ahikam, Shafan's son, or the princes
who let Baruch go to join Jeremiah before bringing the
scroll to the king, or the three who vainly asked the king
not to destroy the scroll [1]—did these or other friends perhaps persuade Jehoiakim that Jeremiah after all should
be allowed to speak for his God? That may be what happened—Jeremiah was not without friends—but there is
no record. How he could safely speak again is unknown;
that he spoke is certain.

The paragraph at the beginning of chapter 20 tells of
his speaking and the consequences:

> Pashhur, Immer's son, the priest, being the officer in charge
> of God's house, heard Jeremiah prophesy these words
> (20:1).

What Pashhur heard was such words as had already all
but cost Jeremiah his life—he never learned. His new
offense is described in the preceding chapter (19). Jeremiah had acted out part of his message; he had taken a
pottery jug to the city dump and smashed it and said that
God would thus break up his people and city irreparably.[2]
He had also referred to the valley Ge-hinnom outside the
city wall, the place where children were offered by fire
to Baal (in another passage in Jeremiah, he is called
Molech),[3] and had said that the city itself would become
just such a hell for its inhabitants.[4] Isaiah had expressed
the same thought. He had spoken of Jerusalem as a fur-
nace of God [5] and as an 'ari'el, a place for burning sacri-

---

[1] Jer. 26:17, 24; 36:19, 25.
[2] Jer. 19:1, 2a, 10, 11a.
[3] Jer. 32:35.
[4] Jer. 19:4, 5, 12, 13.
[5] Isa. 31:9.

fices,[6] with its people the victims—Isaiah had spoken thus
and had not been molested.

When, however, Pashhur heard Jeremiah prophesy
these words he

> flogged the prophet Jeremiah and he put him in the stocks
> which were in the upper Benjamin gate of God's house and
> [he] released Jeremiah from the stocks on the following
> day (20:2-3a).

The Hebrew word translated "stocks" is from the verb,
which also means to overturn. Apparently the stocks held
the prisoner bent and added physical pain to the indignity involved. If this occurred near the end of Jehoiakim's
reign, around 600, Jeremiah would then have been about
fifty years old.

This experience, too, did not deflect him from his prophetic course. When Pashhur released him Jeremiah said:

> "God has not named you Pashhur but *magor missaviv*
> [horror round about]" (v. 3b),

and he held out for Pashhur the expectation of a series of
such atrocities as those with which Amos long before
under similar circumstances had threatened the priest
Amaziah in Beth-el.[7]

A few years later—it was after 598 when king Jehoiachin and many people of Jerusalem had been taken captive to Babylonia (the first deportation)—Jeremiah was
again threatened with torture, threatened but spared. He
had written a letter to the exiles in Babylonia and had said
things which angered the prophet Shemaiah there. Then
Shemaiah wrote to the priest Zephaniah in Jerusalem:

---

[6] Isa. 29:1-2; see Blank, *Prophetic Faith in Isaiah*, p. 4.
[7] Jer. 20:4-6; compare Amos 7:17.

"God has made you priest in place of the priest Jehoiada in charge of God's house. You should put in stocks and collar any mad man [*meshugga'*] who prophesies. Now why have you not rebuked Jeremiah of Anathoth who prophesies to you, inasmuch as he has sent word to us in Babylonia: 'It will be long. Build houses and inhabit them. Plant gardens and eat their produce'" (29:26-28).

But Zephaniah was more friendly to Jeremiah than Pashhur had been in his place, and instead of rebuking and abusing Jeremiah, he merely read the letter to him (v. 29). The tone of his voice as he read aloud Shemaiah's letter is not reported, nor whether he chuckled over the epithet *meshugga'*, or raised an admonitory finger.

The next dated event in the biography is described in chapters 27 and 28. It is an encounter between Jeremiah and a prophet who disputed his authority. It occurred in the reign of Zedekiah.[8]

Zedekiah was courting trouble. Viewed realistically, he was subject to Babylonia, a puppet king. When Nebuchadrezzar had deposed Jehoiachin and carried him off he set up Zedekiah in his stead,[9] and Judah became a tributary state within the great king's realm. Poetically, though with confusion of natural processes, the prophet Ezekiel at this same time described the political situation in a parable of eagles and cedar trees. (The explanations in parentheses are Ezekiel's own; they are taken from his chapter, but there they are grouped at the conclusion of the parable.)

3. The great eagle, with great wings, long pinions,
     Full feathered, brightly colored, came to the Lebanon,

[8] See First Additional Note, p. 234.
[9] II Kings 24:8-17.

Took the crown of the cedar, (4) plucked its top shoot,
Brought it to a land of commerce, set it out in a merchant city.

12b.   ([That is to say:] The king of Babylon came to Jerusalem,
Took her king [Jehoiachin] and her princes,
And brought them along to Babylonia.)

5.   And he took of the seed of the land and set it out in a plant nursery
. . . By plentiful water he set it out as a willow

6a.   [That it might] sprout and become a low spreading vine
Its tendrils turning to him, its roots beneath him.

13a.   ([That is to say:] He took one of the royal seed [Zedekiah] and made a pact with him . . .

14.   To be a lowly kingdom, without ambitions,
To uphold the covenant, for it to stand.)

6b.   So it became a vine, branched, put out runners.

7.   And there was [another] great eagle, with great wings, full feathered.
And this vine bent towards him its roots,
Reached out its branches towards him, [for him] to water it in the nursery . . .

15.   ([That is to say: Zedekiah] revolted against [Nebuchadrezzar], sending emissaries to Egypt
For horses and troops.
Will it succeed? Will one who does such things prosper? . . .)

(Ezek. 17:3-7, 12b-15.)

This was Ezekiel's poetic way of saying that Zedekiah's only sane policy was to acknowledge his ties to Babylonia and remain tributary. Now if as a Jewish captive in Babylonia Ezekiel was informed as to Zedekiah's unrest, the news of it could hardly fail to claim the attention also of the great king.

And in Jerusalem at the same time Jeremiah evinced concern. He constituted himself a public demonstration, went about in bonds and fetters, gave the royal emissaries bonds and fetters to carry back to Edom, Moab, Ammon, Tyre, Sidon, for their respective kings. They should know by this symbol that they were bondsmen to Babylon, destined to wear the yoke. He gave the same counsel to his own king Zedekiah: Wear the yoke of the Babylonian king. The prophets are false who counsel revolt.[10]

When Jeremiah called those other prophets false he stepped quite heavily upon certain people's toes. Prominent among those whom he offended was Hananiah, the prophet from Gibeon. According to that prophet God said: "I have broken the yoke of Babylon's king!" (28:2) and said, too, that he would in short order—"in two years"—return to Jerusalem the temple vessels, Jehoiachin, and all of the exiles whom Nebuchadrezzar had carried away (28:4 f.). Between Jeremiah and Hananiah the difference was as black and white. There was no middle ground—each was saying the other lied. There were words between them, a prelude to violence. Impulsively at first Jeremiah responded with an "Amen!"

"Amen! So may God do! Let God but fulfill the words of your prophecy and bring back from Babylon to this place

[10] Jer. 27.

the vessels [taken as loot] from God's house, and all of
the exiles . . ." (28:6).

Then more soberly he said:

> "Yet hear the word that I say to you and the whole people:
> The prophets who have been of old—before you and before
> me—prophesied for many lands and great kingdoms of war,
> disaster, and disease. Any prophet who prophesies good,
> only when what he says occurs is it known that God has
> really sent that prophet" (28:7-9).

Hananiah recognized the taunt and challenge in Jeremiah's words and he made a fist.

> The prophet Hananiah took the yoke from the neck of
> Jeremiah the prophet and he broke it. And Hananiah said
> before all the people: "So God said, Thus I will break the
> yoke of Nebuchadrezzar king of Babylon, in two years time,
> from the neck of all the nations" (28:10-11a).

Faced with this show of violence, Jeremiah walked away.
But after a while, the biographer tells, God sent him back
to Hananiah with a further word: "You have broken bars
of wood only to make way for bars of iron" (11b-13).

This encounter between Jeremiah and Hananiah is
significant for reasons yet to be considered, but in the
present context it stands as one more episode in the succession of indignities and torments in the life of Jeremiah.

A number of such circumstances, concentrated in chapters 37 and 38, cluster about the final years of Jerusalem,
588 and 587. As Jeremiah had foreseen, Zedekiah's policy
brought the Babylonians again to the gates of Jerusalem,
and for two years, with a brief interruption only, the city

was in a state of siege, and Jeremiah was involved in the commotion. Considering the things he said and did in this time of crisis for Jerusalem, what is surprising is not that Jeremiah experienced grave difficulties but that he survived at all. People who did not share his religious position could quite readily have supposed that he was "giving aid and comfort to the enemy." His position might seem ambiguous, to say the least, and the unsympathetic might brand him a traitor.

In a concise narrative at the beginning of chapter 21, and again in another at the end of chapter 37, the king Zedekiah asks counsel of Jeremiah. The two narratives are not different versions of the same incident; the king consulted him on these separate occasions. There is indeed a similarity between them, that on both occasions the Babylonian army stood before the gates of Jerusalem; the city was in a state of siege. But there is also this difference between them, that in the first, Jeremiah appears to be at liberty, whereas he is confined to prison in the second. Between the one and the other appearance of Jeremiah before the king, the prophet had been arrested, flogged, and imprisoned; but this change in his fortunes made little difference—he was no less outspoken when he replied to the king the second time.

According to the narrative (in 37:11-16), Jeremiah's arrest occurred during the temporary absence of the besieging army. The forces of Pharaoh which came up from Egypt into the southland created a temporary diversion; Nebuchadrezzar withdrew to meet the danger on his flank and Jerusalem had respite. It was in that interval between the first and the final phases of the siege that Jeremiah lost his liberty.[11] But Zedekiah consulted him

---

[11] See below, pp. 50 f.

both before the siege was interrupted and after it was resumed. What appears in chapter 21 passed between king and prophet in that initial phase of the siege. So we may infer from the fact that there the narrator says nothing of Jeremiah's confinement.

Nebuchadrezzar fulfilled Jeremiah's prediction and came to punish the defection of Judah. Jeremiah had been right, as the king had to recognize, and now the king sent to ask him what next—to ask and to be rebuffed.

> The word which Jeremiah had from God when king Zedekiah sent Pashhur, Malkiyah's son, and Zephaniah, the priest, Maaseyah's son, to say: "Apply to God on our behalf, because Nebuchadrezzar, king of Babylon, is making war on us. Perhaps God will act for us according to all his wonders and [Nebuchadrezzar] will go from us." But Jeremiah said to them: "Say thus to Zedekiah: 'So said the Lord, the God of Israel: I will turn about the weapons of war in your hands which you are employing against the king of Babylon, [them] and the Chaldaeans who are besieging you without the wall, and will bring them right into the city. And I too will fight with you with an outstretched hand and a strong arm and with anger and with indignation and with great wrath, and will smite the inhabitants of this city, both man and beast. They will die of a grievous plague. And after that . . . I will give Zedekiah, king of Judah, and his servants . . . over to Nebuchadrezzar, king of Babylon . . . and he will put them to the sword without mercy, without pity, without compassion'" (21:1-7).

The king cradled a wistful hope which the prophet coldly shattered. When, in ages past, similar prospects threatened this people, God had often hastened to aid them, and his arm outstretched with power reduced the Pharaoh or routed the Canaanite. In many a past crisis God's wonders

had converted a sure defeat into a national triumph, and
the young Zedekiah with his kind of piety wondered
whether perhaps a new miracle was taking form in the
mind of God. "Perhaps, '*ulai* . . . ?"

Against him Jeremiah loosed a cold wind of reality.
In a feat of prophetic irony he let an ambiguity tantalize
his questioner until he was ready to resolve it into a terrifying certainty. In Hebrew, as in the translation, the
expression "to fight with" is ambiguous and can mean "as
an ally along with" or "as an enemy against." It is only
the end of God's sentence which decides: "And I too will
fight with you, with an outstretched hand and a strong
arm and with anger and with indignation and with great
wrath, and will smite [—smite whom?] the inhabitants of
this city . . . And . . . I will give Zedekiah . . . over to
. . . the king of Babylon . . . and he will put him to
the sword without mercy, without pity, without compassion." The last words match the earlier words now with
new force: ". . . with anger and with indignation and
with great wrath . . . without mercy, without pity, without compassion." And ambiguity has given way to horror.

Economy of words distinguishes the drama of the second
interview. One verse suffices to set the scene and to ring
the curtain down.

King Zedekiah sent and took him. And the king asked him
secretly in his house and said: "Is there a word from God?"
And Jeremiah said: "There is," and said: "You will fall into
the hands of the king of Babylon" (37:17).

The young king and the aging prophet came face to face.
Zedekiah would have been about thirty-two at the time,[12]

[12] II Kings 24:18.

Jeremiah in his early sixties. Though young, the king was king; though in the presence of his king, the prophet was prophet. Was it that Jeremiah had been doubly right— right that the Babylonians would come, right again that they would resume the interrupted siege? Or was it that in him some natural dignity and nobility of purpose combined with the weight of his years to suggest immunity? Whatever it was that gave him the liberty, Jeremiah spoke out. Neither king nor prophet wasted words in courtly language. The king went straight to the point and he got a straight answer: "Is there a word from God?" "There is. You will fall into the hands of the king of Babylon."

Perhaps uneasy because Jeremiah was sure, and certainly uneasy because he, Zedekiah, knew that he was in revolt against his lord the king of Babylon, the puppet king can not have heard the prophet's words unshaken. If his imagination revealed even a part of what was to befall, he had cause to shudder and his skin must creep. It was not a matter of war games between the two kings, and Zedekiah's defeat meant tragedy. When he was captured—as he was, because Jeremiah still was right and Jerusalem fell—he was not simply killed, or simply carried away as a captive to an alien land. He was plundered. The great king his captor Nebuchadrezzar took his sight from him. But before he put out Zedekiah's eyes he gave him a memory. The last that he saw was the execution of the child princes, his children, his hope. Then he descended into a life of darkness.

We know of Zedekiah's fate because it is on record. Jeremiah could not, of course, foresee it in the fullness of its horror. But he was not treating the king to rhetoric or playing with quaint phrases when he said of him: "You will fall into the hands of the king of Babylon."

It may be that Zedekiah was beaten and silent; at any rate, Jeremiah stayed with him to point a moral and to ask a favor. His moral had the form of a taunt: "Where are your prophets who prophesied: the king of Babylon will not come in against you and this land?" And his request was a protestation: "What have I done to you and your servants and this people that you have put me in prison?" and a plea: "Now hear, my lord, O king; accept my petition and do not send me back to the house of Jonathan the scribe, to die there." The king assenting, Jeremiah was transferred to the "court of the guard" and assigned a daily loaf of bread from "the street of the bakers" as long as bread was to be had in the city.[13]

[13] Jer. 37:18-21.

IV

The Last Days of Jerusalem

The postlude to the second interview affords the incidental information that Jeremiah's imprisonment en-
dangered his life. How did he come to prison, and what
occurred there? Several events from the months in 587
that preceded the fall of Jerusalem make reference to his
confinement. Chapters 37 and 38 describe these events,
and chapter 34 narrates a striking episode which may
have set the stage for his arrest.

When the lords of Jerusalem betrayed their Hebrew
slaves Jeremiah "got down to cases." He had spoken much
in principle; now here was a flagrant violation of all that
held meaning for him, and he lifted his voice and decried
a specific offense committed by known offenders. It was
an event which occurred when the Babylonian army withdrew to meet the threat from Egypt. The narrative begins
with 34:8, goes on to the end of that chapter, and probably
resumes in 37:7b-10. The scene is laid in the last verses
of the thirty-fourth chapter (the army of Babylon's king
has gone but God will bring it back) and in 37:7
(Pharaoh's army which has come out to help you will go
back home). The absence of the Babylonian army was the

46

occasion for the betrayal. Earlier, the lords of Jerusalem had done the right thing. First they did what was right and then they reversed it, and that was betrayal, and a profanation of God's name.

Whether they did it for right reasons or for wrong reasons the lords of Jerusalem for once did the right thing as Jeremiah saw the right: they freed their Hebrew slaves. We might suspect that their doing so was a manifestation of what has been called "fox-hole religion"—a kind of last-ditch measure in a time of peril. We might suspect that it was so; their impulse was born while the Babylonians were pounding on the gates of Jerusalem, and it barely outlived the peril. The account vaguely alludes to a motivation; "you turned today and did what pleased me" (34:15), God says to those slaveholders in Jerusalem. Though this may mean "it pleased me for whatever reason you did it," it probably means "you did what you did in order to please me."

Why did they think that it would please God? Because Jeremiah had been urging it? Because, after all, according to the pact that God had made with their fathers when he brought them from Egypt it was obligatory [1]—even though neither they nor their fathers had got around to discharging the obligation as yet? And did other, possibly unavowed "practical" motives mingle with the wish to please God? Were provisions running low in the larger households of the besieged city, and might it be better for the family (charity begins at home) if the slaves were sent out to shift for themselves? Or might it be argued that freed men, having more at stake personally, would make better soldiers?

[1] See Deut. 15:12-18 and Exod. 21:1-11. The Jeremiah passage has reference to the deuteronomic formulation of the law with its reference also to female slaves.

It was agreed and decided and done—done with noise and ceremony. First came the proclamation; they proclaimed liberty one to the other, master to Hebrew slave. Then, in the temple in Jerusalem, the king and princes participating, a solemn ritual! They "cut" a covenant. A calf was led in and slaughtered, butchered, and divided down the middle. One half was laid over against the other with a passage between them—so we may infer from what little is told here, and from Abram's ceremony and the attendant nightly vision in Genesis 15—and then the covenanters walked the blood-sprinkled path between the pieces. Probably, too, the agreement was read aloud; and whether he spoke it or not each participant knew as he walked that path that he took on himself a conditional curse. If he failed to carry out his undertaking, in this grisly fashion he, too, would be butchered.

It was a solemn and awesome procedure, but the lords of Jerusalem walked the path with tongue in cheek. In the jubilation which ensued when the Babylonians broke camp the severed calf was forgotten. And then, sober once more, the princes looked around and began to rue their impulsive generosity. A new proclamation: they revoked the freedom they had given. And that was the betrayal.

Jeremiah called it a "profanation of God's name." It may be that he found the phrase, made it especially to characterize the offense. It is not clearly attested earlier in biblical literature, but it was to become a classic phrase.[2]

Jeremiah called the treachery of the lords of Jerusalem a profanation of God's name, and in unrestrained fury and uncontrolled language he described the fate which they had brought near. Now, assuredly, the Babylonians will return and take Jerusalem and butcher the treacherous

---

[2] See Blank, *Prophetic Faith in Isaiah*, pp. 122-23.

inhabitants. Here follows in a slightly abbreviated form the narrator's story of the betrayal:

The word that Jeremiah had from God after king Zedekiah had made a pact with the whole people in Jerusalem for them to proclaim liberty, for each man to set free his Hebrew slave and each his Hebrew slave-girl, not to hold them in bondage, no man [to hold in bondage] a Jew his brother. And all of the princes and the whole people who had entered into the pact, for each man to set free his slave and each his slave-girl, not to hold them longer in bondage, listened—listened and freed them.

But they turned, after that, and took back the slaves and slave-girls whom they had set free, and bound them again as slaves and slave-girls.

And God's word came from God to Jeremiah: So said the Lord, the God of Israel: . . . You turned today and did what pleased me, proclaiming liberty one to the other, and concluded a pact in my presence, in the house dedicated to me. And then you turned about and profaned my name, taking back each one his slave and each his slave-girl whom you had set free . . . and binding them again to serve you as slaves and slave-girls.

So then thus God has said: You did not listen to me to proclaim liberty each to his brother and to each other; lo, I proclaim for you, God says, liberty—to sword, disease and famine, and I will make you an object of horror to all the kingdoms of the earth and will make the men who concluded the pact with me, who did not keep the terms of the pact which they made in my presence, [like] the calf which they divided, to walk between its parts, the princes of Judah and princes of Jerusalem, the officials and the priests and all the people of the land, who walked between the parts of the calf. And I will deliver them over to their enemies, to those that seek their life, and their dead bodies shall be food for the fowl of heaven and the beasts of the earth. And I will deliver Zedekiah, king of Judah, and his princes over to their enemies and to those that seek their life and to the army of the king of Babylon which has gone from you. Lo, I give command, God says, and bring them back to this city, and they shall war against it and take it and burn it, and I will make the cities of Judah an uninhabited desolation. . . . Do not deceive yourselves and think: The Chaldaeans have left us for good; for they are not gone. For, if you had smitten all the army of the Chaldaeans who are warring with you and [only] wounded men were left of them, they would arise, each in his tent, and burn this city (34:8-22; 37:7-10).

That is the story of the betrayal.

Not long after this event Jeremiah was arrested. There is no clear connection between the one occurrence and the other, though surely Jeremiah's denunciation of the influential Jerusalemites for their perfidy made him no friends among them. Perhaps the climate soured to the degree that any false move on his part would seem to be a provocation. This is what happened:

It occurred, while the Chaldaean forces were absent from Jerusalem because of the army of Pharaoh, that Jeremiah started from Jerusalem towards the territory of Benjamin to get possession of a field there among the people, and when he reached the Benjamin gate where a captain of the guard was stationed, Yiriyyah son of Shelemyah, Hananiah's son, by name, [the captain] arrested the prophet Jeremiah, saying: "You are deserting to the Chaldaeans." But Jeremiah said: "It is untrue; I am not deserting to the Chaldaeans." Paying no heed to him, Yiriyyah arrested Jeremiah and brought him before the princes. And the princes were enraged at him and whipped him and committed him to prison in the house of Jonathan the scribe, for they had made his house a prison. [In this manner] Jeremiah came to the house of the pit and to the vaults and Jeremiah remained there many days (37:11-16).

There is Jeremiah's own word for it that the accusation was false. "It is untrue," he said; "I am not deserting to the Chaldaeans." And the narrator also did not believe that he was deserting; according to his account, Jeremiah was on his way to his home country Benjamin (he was born in Anathoth which was in Benjamin)[3] "to get possession of a field there." It was perhaps not strange, however, that his move was misconstrued. His recent insistence that the Babylonians would take the city with ease and butcher its inhabitants could only strengthen the impression which he must have given a few years earlier, that his sympathies were with Nebuchadrezzar. How else would most of the men of Jerusalem have interpreted his wearing the yoke of Babylon's king?[4] Their conclusion was not wholly unreasonable. But animosity played its part as well: "The princes were enraged at him and whipped him"—this had happened before, when he was a younger man—"and committed him to prison. . . ."

So Jeremiah came to prison. That was the prison from which Zedekiah had him brought when he asked him a second time for word from God, the prison from which Jeremiah begged the king to release him: "Do not send me back to the house of Jonathan the scribe, to die there." What special danger lurked in that house is not revealed, unless the words translated "pit" and "vaults" suggest the unwholesome atmosphere of a dungeon. Whatever the

[3] Jer. 1:1; see below, pp. 77 f.
[4] See above, p. 39.

threat to his life, the prophet so feared it that he could bring himself to ask the favor. Moreover, the king recognized the reasonableness of his plea, since he ordered the prophet to the court of the guard and assigned him a daily loaf while the food lasted.[5]

Jeremiah could breathe again—and speak. He had an audience in the court of the guard and when the occasion offered he spoke out, undismayed by his prison experience. There was occasion: the Pharaoh returned to his Egypt and Babylon's king returned to the siege of Jerusalem. And again in the ensuing crisis what Jeremiah said brought him into mortal danger. He made an important statement, which seems, remarkably, to be quoted in four different places, though nowhere in full.[6] According to his accusers what he said was this:

> So God has said: Whoever remains in this city will die by the sword, by famine, or by disease. But whoever goes over to the Chaldaeans will live and his life will be his reward . . . (38:2).

And again:

> So God has said: This city will be handed over to the forces of Babylon's king and he will take it (38:3).

That much of Jeremiah's statement is quoted in the thirty-eighth chapter. In chapter 21 there is a preface to each of the two items:

> So God has said: I offer you a way of life and a way of death: Whoever remains in this city, [etc.]

[5] Jer. 37:17-21, considered above, pp. 43-45.
[6] Buttenwieser, *The Prophets of Israel,* pp. 69-76, has noted how 38:2, 3; 21:8-10; 34:2, 3; and 32:3-5 are related.

as in the foregoing passage; and then, leading into the other threat,

> For I have turned my gaze upon this city for ill and not for good, God says; it will be handed over to Babylon's king and he will destroy it by fire (21:8-10).

When again the statement is quoted, in the thirty-fourth chapter, God's special word to Zedekiah is included:

> I am handing this city over to Babylon's king and he will destroy it by fire. And you yourself will not escape him, but you will be caught and handed over to him and your eyes will look into the eyes of Babylon's king and you will speak with him mouth to mouth and will come to Babylon (34:2, 3).

As finally the address is cited in chapter 32:3-5, in addition to the threats already listed it contains the concluding words:

> If you fight the Chaldaeans you will not succeed (32:5).

In view of such an expression on the part of the prophet the defenders of Jerusalem were perhaps entitled to their opinion that Jeremiah was impeding the war effort.

The narrator in chapter 38 relates that certain personages heard the prophet speak these words to the people and that the princes then said to the king:

> "This man must die, because by speaking such words to them he is weakening the hands of the soldiers left in this city and the hands of the whole population. Indeed, this man desires not the welfare of this people but their ruin" (38:4).

This time there was no trial. The king washed his hands
of the affair:

> "He is yours," King Zedekiah said. "With you the king can
> do nothing."
>   So they took Jeremiah and put him into the cistern of
> the king's son Malkiyyah in the court of the guard. They
> let Jeremiah down with ropes. There was no water in the
> cistern, only mud; but Jeremiah sank into the mud (38:5 f.).

The prophet is back where he was. If he had reason to
fear for his life in the pit in the house of the scribe he
has all the more reason now to fear in the mire at the
bottom of a shaft.

It is not reported how many hours (or days) Jeremiah
remained there waiting for death before he arose as though
from the tomb, but a friend again intervened and saved
him. This time it was an officer, an Ethiopian called Eved-
melech, who for some reason cared what happened to
Jeremiah and who at the same time, fortunately, had ac-
cess to the king. He was in the palace when he learned
that they had put Jeremiah in the deep cistern. But the
king was at the Benjamin gate. So Eved-melech went
from the palace to find the king, and to him he said:

> "My lord, O King, these men have dealt wrongly in all they
> have done to Jeremiah the prophet, putting him into the
> cistern where he is sure to die" [7] (38:9).

All the fight seems to have gone from Zedekiah. When
the princes insisted he must silence Jeremiah he agreed,
apathetic, and when Eved-melech, deploring their action,
urged the rescue of the prophet he again assented, re-

---

[7] Reading so, with a change of vowels, instead of "and he died there."

versing his position—he authorized Eved-melech to save
Jeremiah from death.

> So the king told Eved-melech the Ethiopian: "Take along
> three [8] men and raise the prophet Jeremiah from the cistern
> before he dies" (v. 10).

Jeremiah's benefactor made preparations for the rescue.
He took along rags and let them down with ropes to
Jeremiah. Padding his armpits against the pull, Jeremiah
adjusted the ropes, and the four men hoisted him from
the cistern—out of the depths again into the comparative
freedom of the court of the guard, where he was allowed
to remain until Jerusalem fell.[9]

In the interval between his rescue and the fall of Jerusalem, according to the record, two things occurred: Jeremiah rewarded his friend, and he bought a field. He rewarded Eved-melech with a promise:

> So the Lord of hosts, Israel's God, has said: I am carrying
> out my word against this city, for ill and not for good . . .
> But I will rescue you on that day, God says, and you will not
> be handed over to the men whom you dread, and I will
> let you escape and you will not fall by the sword; your life
> will be your reward—because you trusted me, God says
> (39:16-18).

It was "a life for a life"; for saving his life Jeremiah promised life to Eved-melech. God, he said, would reward his
"trust," and nothing but this man's concern for Jeremiah
now puts content into the phrase "because you trusted
me." Or, better put, Eved-melech's service to Jeremiah

[8] So, instead of "thirty," as the form of the next Hebrew word suggests.
[9] Jer. 38:11-13, 28.

is the only preserved evidence that he "trusted God." If
the record is complete and nothing else is intended, then
his trust means that, as the rare individual in his generation, he took Jeremiah's prophetic word at face value,
believed that in his prophet God was speaking, and accepted what he said. If so, his motivation was not unlike
that of the court, which refused to speak a death sentence
for Jeremiah when he had announced, in God's name, the
destruction of the temple. Twice then the prophet escaped
death because of the trust of certain men.[10] Twice also
Jeremiah spoke a word of human warmth to a friend, here
to Eved-melech, as on an earlier occasion to Baruch, who
also risked much on his behalf.[11]

Still in that interval before the fall of Jerusalem Jeremiah bought a field. The story is told in 32:1-15. It gets
under way in the sixth verse with the description of a
premonition which he had.

> I had God's word: Hanamel, the son of your uncle Shallum
> will come to you and say: "Purchase my field in Anathoth
> because yours is the kinsman's right" (32:6-7).

When his cousin came to him in the court of the guard
as he had foreseen, "I knew," he says, "that it was God's
word, and I bought the field" (vv. 8b-9a). At that darkest
moment in Jerusalem's history, when no one was more
sure than he that Jerusalem would fall, and a few months
only before it did fall, Jeremiah did what must have
seemed a wholly irrational thing: he bought the field—
with no present hope of possessing it. In fact, he made a
show of the transaction so that it would not escape public

[10] See above, pp. 21, 24.
[11] See above, p. 32, and below, pp. 144 f., 211.

notice and would even be on record for times to come.
And he explained his strange behavior.

> And I bought the field from Hanamel, the son of my uncle
> in Anathoth, and weighed out the silver for him, the seven-
> teen shekels of silver, and I made a record of it and sealed
> it before witnesses, weighing out the silver on scales. And
> I took the deed of purchase (the sealed one . . . together
> with the open one) and gave the deed to Baruch . . . in
> the presence of Hanamel, my uncle['s son], and the wit-
> nesses who signed the deed, [and] in the presence of all
> the Judeans in the court of the guard, and charged Baruch
> before them . . . : "Take these deeds, the sealed one and
> the open one, and put them in an earthen jar, that they may
> last for many days."
>
> For so the Lord of hosts, Israel's God, has said: Fields
> and vineyards shall yet be purchased in this land (vv.
> 9-15).

Jeremiah was not, apparently, thinking of the near future,
because he made the same sort of provision for preserving
the deeds of purchase as was effective in preserving the
Dead Sea scrolls for many centuries; he put them in
earthen jars. That at some future time, but not too soon,
fields would be possessed again in the land, he was confident, and he expressed his trust in this tangible fashion
and "went on record." It is notable that the two convictions lived in him together at that time: the obsession that
Jerusalem was doomed and the confidence that after a
while settled life in the land would be possible again.

There is no further reference to the imprisonment of
Jeremiah beyond the note that when Jerusalem fell Babylonian officers took him from the court of the guard and
gave him in the care of Gedaliah, the new puppet governor

of the fragment of a community which remained. This
is told in the thirty-ninth chapter:

> And Nebuchadrezzar, Babylon's king, gave charge concern-
> ing Jeremiah to Nebuzaradan, the captain of the guards:
> "Take him and have him under your care and do him no
> harm, but do with him as he says." So Nebuzaradan . . .
> sent and took Jeremiah from the court of the guard and
> brought him to Gedaliah . . . (39:11-14).

The biographer has not much more to tell of Jeremiah's
life. The fate of Gedaliah and of the community that
gathered about him, related in chapters 40 and 41, is only
incidentally Jeremiah's story. Jeremiah becomes involved
again when, after the murder of Gedaliah, the remnants
of the community consult him as they prepare to seek
safety in Egypt. This is told in chapters 42 and 43. The
frightened survivors approached him with a show of respect; he had been grimly right.

> "Let our petition sway you, and pray to the Lord your God
> on our behalf and for all of this remnant, for we remain a
> few out of many as you see us; so may the Lord your God
> tell us of the way we should go and what we should do"
> (42:2 f.).

Jeremiah agreed, promised to report to them the whole
of God's word for them when he himself learned of it,
whereupon, unprompted, they swore a sacred oath:

> "God be a true and faithful witness to our oath: We will
> do according to all [the word with] which the Lord your
> God sends you to us!" (42:5).

It is significant that Jeremiah gave no immediate reply.
He really did consult his God and listen long for the in-

sight which he must communicate to the would-be emi-
grants.[12] It was only "after ten days" (v. 7) that he brought
back to them the word of God.

Then he brought an unexpected word: It was now
God's will that they remain in the land. God was ready
to plant them here again—and not uproot them, and they
needed no more to fear the king of Babylon. God indeed
was determined that now they would remain in the land.
They would be safer here than in Egypt. They must not
leave.[13] The word was unexpected and it was received
with dismayed unbelief. The "scoffers" did not suppress
their indignation.

> "You are lying. The Lord our God did not send you to say:
> You shall not go to Egypt to live. Baruch, Neriyah's son,
> has been disposing you against us . . ." (43:2 f.).

How they ever came to suppose that Baruch had a quarrel
with them, or, if so, that he had such influence over Jeremiah that the prophet would mistake his words for God's,
will remain a mystery. Perhaps their suspicion was a product of hysteria in search of a scapegoat. Equally implausible, of course, is their supposition that Jeremiah was
simply deceiving them. As an Isaiah had observed for
example, people believe what they want to believe and
reject the unwanted as incredible. The solemn promise
which the fugitives made to Jeremiah, expecting God to
approve their flight, was as nothing when he disappointed
them. The prophet could only be lying; the unwanted
counsel was simply false, and they were completely absolved of their oath.

[12] On the matter of listening, see again below, Chap. IX.
[13] Jer. 42:10-22.

The sequel to their rejection of Jeremiah's reply was this: that they abducted Jeremiah, and Baruch as well, and took them willing or not to Egypt,[14] where all along the fugitives had wanted to go. Jeremiah seemed, like Joseph, to have been drawn from the pit only to be carried off to Egypt. Jeremiah, then scarcely less than seventy years of age, again a kind of prisoner, came to Egypt to finish his days, to a land for which he had shown no love. The biographer knows nothing to tell of his death, but he does record one encounter—it might almost be called a squabble—between the prophet and the refugee women in Egypt.

It makes up the greater part of the forty-fourth chapter. Jeremiah is no longer the respected reprover of kings, and the women are impertinent, saucy. What the Judean fugitives were doing in Egypt was, in Jeremiah's opinion, simply suicidal. They were abandoning such loyalty to their God as had survived and were going on alien ways "bringing offerings to foreign gods in Egypt." [15] Jeremiah said aloud what he thought, but he was not unanswered. He was quite used to being heard in tolerant silence; this time the women talked back. Perhaps made bolder by their numbers, "all the women, assembled as a throng" (v. 15), replied:

> "The word that you speak to us in God's name—we do not hear you. We are going to do according to the word that comes from our mouth, bringing offerings to the queen of heaven and pouring out libations to her . . ." (44:16 f.).

Of course, the colloquy did not end there; Jeremiah yet said for God:

[14] Jer. 43:4-7.
[15] Jer. 44:7 f.

"The remnant of Judah who came to Egypt to live will learn whose word prevails, theirs or mine . . ." (44:28b).

The incident ends with his retort, and there is nothing besides this incident to tell of his last days in Egypt.[16]

The narratives about Jeremiah, the biographical sections of his book surveyed on the foregoing pages in their presumed chronological order, describe a prophet's desolating career. Peril and the experience of violence, indignity, and virtual banishment were among the ingredients of his life. They are there in his biography; we have read this catalogue of misery: He was accused and tried for a capital offense and though he obtained acquittal he was to hear of a like-minded prophet who, for the same offense, did not escape death. He spent years as an outcast and learned of the obliteration of his book. When a king ordered his arrest he had to prolong his hiding. Active again he was taken and flogged and endured the worse pain of exposure in stocks. A rival prophet assaulted him, another wrote calumny and urged further violence. An official accused him falsely so that he was flogged again and imprisoned. Prison life threatened his health, confinement in the depths of a cistern threatened him with extinction. Delivered from that danger he yet remained under arrest. He was released whcn his king suffered defeat, but only to be abducted to Egypt, to spend his last years as an *émigré*.

. . . They entreated him evil, who nevertheless was a prophet, sanctified in his mother's womb that he might

[16] Concerning the threats to Egypt in 43:8-13 and 44:30, see Fourth Additional Note, p. 241.

root out, and afflict, and destroy; and that he might build
up also, and plant (Ecclus. 49:7, Apoc.).

To be sure, the biography is not a tale of unrelieved
misery. Friends appear in the hostile crowd; moments of
triumph alternate with defeat; he dares now and then to
think hopeful thoughts. Though it might have seemed
that every hand was against him, he was not quite friend-
less. There were the elders who defended him at the trial
along with a certain Ahikam; there was Baruch who joined
him in hiding, wrote the book, read it publicly, and apparently remained with him until the end in Egypt; there
were the officials at court who protested the burning of
his book; there was the Zephaniah who only read to him
the threatening letter; there was Eved-melech who saved
his life; there was even the king, Zedekiah, who, though
he wavered, did not quite desert him, and there was Gedaliah who thought as he did and whom he joined when
Jerusalem fell. He had an occasional triumph. At the trial,
his defense was credited; his prediction was right that the
Babylonians would come, right again that they would
return; he was consulted by king and people—twice by
the king—and the king was impressed. He permitted himself a distant hope and bought a field. Nevertheless, according to the biographer, friends, success, and hope did
not play the leading roles in his dramatic life.

Now, the biographer, though doubtless sympathetic to
his subject, produced a quite objective report. As Jeremiah's biographer left it, the biblical account is notable for
the reporter's detachment. Any note of indignation on the
prophet's behalf is an importation in the modern retelling
here in this book. The biographer could, of course, have
related the events with a bias either way, favoring either

the suffering prophet or the society which made him its victim.

Something could well be said for the society which tried to silence Jeremiah. Start with the persuasion that speaking calamity produces calamity, and a man with Jeremiah's evil tidings becomes a menace to society. Or, without superstition, posit a nation at war or a city besieged; in such a situation a Jeremiah predicting defeat and advocating surrender appears to be working for the enemy. Moreover, Jeremiah questioned what had always been "true," questioned the authority of other priests and impugned the honesty of other prophets, assessed blame freely and made demands in God's name; he was beyond doubt a "disturber of the peace." If a public figure takes no care to say the unpleasant in words that do not offend, and if instead he must insult, threaten, and upset everyone, he must expect to make enemies. Society was in self-defense, compelled to treat a menacing Jeremiah as it did—compelled to exclude, isolate, quarantine such a one, as a proper security measure. What society was not compelled to do and yet did was to let Jeremiah live (witness the fate of Uriah) and allow him to speak as he spoke, despite the threat in his words. And it is a marvel that he survived and a perpetual marvel that his words survived, and a tribute to the tolerance of the people of Judah in his day. An astounding phenomenon in the history of human tolerance is the survival of the disconcerting message of the Hebrew prophets.

Factually told as they are in the biographical sections, the events in Jeremiah's life are sad enough. But they are lifted to a new degree of intensity when the prophet himself plays the accompaniment. For in other parts of Jere-

miah's book the biographer's objective statement yields,
and the subjective record appears of Jeremiah's suffering,
his own description of the pain, the doubts, and the emotions that arose in him as the events unfolded. It is the
same story, told now from the point of view of the victim.

Section II

Documents of Self-Revelation

V

How Jeremiah Surrendered to God

The opening chapter of Jeremiah, his "consecration vision," is that one of his documents of self-revelation which refers to the earliest moment in his prophetic life. The literature contains a number of such narratives—those in which a prophet describes his initial experience—and there is a ponderable similarity among them. It is a document of prime importance for the understanding of prophecy in general and Jeremiah in particular.

The consecration vision is the prophet's surrender. From Amos to Ezekiel, one prophet after another describes his call—tells how God took him—possessed him. Amos tells his story with the utmost simplicity. When the priest Amaziah grew alarmed and flexed his muscles and demanded that Amos hold his peace and go on away, the prophet turned wide eyes upon this priest and said, in effect: Oh, don't you know about me? I was very quietly going about my business with the trees and the flocks with no thought of speaking for him when suddenly God took me. "God took me," Amos said, ". . . and told me: Go, prophesy to my people Israel" (Amos 7:14 f.). And it may have been at about the same time, after he had thus spoken to Ama-

ziah, that Amos also drew his analogy and asked: "If a
lion roars who does not fear? If the Lord God has spoken
who will not prophesy?" (Amos 3:8). And his analogy
compared the prophet's activity to the reflex of fear—automatic almost, and beyond the prophet's control.

The statement by Amos is the extreme statement of
his position. Other prophets referred to their surrender
and did so in similar but less emphatic terms. Nearly all
of them said it. Isaiah described his surrender as a central
motif in his vision. This man whose lips fire had first
purified heard God's challenging query: Whom shall I
send? and at once volunteered: "I am ready; send me
then." Whereupon God said: Go, and speak to this people
(Isa. 6:8 f.).

Jeremiah also had his vision, and Ezekiel had his. And
their mouths, too, became instruments of God's will. Dis-
pensing with preliminaries, God said to Jeremiah: Before
you were born "I adopted you" and designated you my
prophet (1:5). Describing his experience as a young man
when God took him, Jeremiah said:

God put forth his hand and touched my mouth, and God
said to me: Lo, I have put my words in your mouth (1:9).

It was similar with Ezekiel though the preparation was
more elaborate. A fantastic vision of God approaching in
his heavenly chariot introduced the great moment when
he received from God's hand a scroll "inscribed on both
sides with moaning and lamentation and woe" and devoured it at God's command, thus symbolically taking into
himself the very words which at suitable times his mouth
would utter (Ezek. 1:4-3:4).

Like Amos, to whom obedience seemed as natural as

his fright at the roar of a lion, and like Isaiah, who readily
volunteered when the word offered, Ezekiel and Jeremiah
acquiesced, surrendered. Ezekiel said that though the
words inscribed on that scroll were bitter, it was in his
mouth "as honey for sweetness" (3:3). And a similar expression appears, not indeed in the first chapter but in
a related context in Jeremiah. "When your words offered,"
he said, "I devoured them; and your word was a joy to
me" (15:16).

So the surrender seems complete, and if there were no
more evidence than this, the conclusion would be justified
that the prophet acquiesced wholly, that God or the spirit
of God took total possession of the person of the prophet
so that the word of God and the word of the prophet were
indistinguishable, that the prophet was one "possessed,"
like Balaam "fallen with opened eyes," [1] or like Saul who
"stripped off his clothes and prophesied . . . and fell
naked [in a trance] all day and night." [2] This much of
what Amos and Isaiah, Jeremiah and Ezekiel have remembered about their "call" leads to the view that they gave
over to God without reserve at least their speech. All of
the visions focus on the mouth. The prophet puts at
God's disposal his organs of articulation. If God is to be
heard by men he must speak the language of men, and in
its primitive formulation that seems to be the definition
of a prophet: one—like Amos, Isaiah, Jeremiah, Ezekiel—
whose mouth God used. The story of Moses is pertinent.
When God proposed to send him to Pharaoh to demand
the release of his people Moses remonstrated. He could
not go, because his speech was thick and hesitant. It was
then that God patiently explained: was it not he, after

[1] Num. 24:4.
[2] I Sam. 19:24.

all, who gave man a mouth? So God simply promised to
"be with" the mouth of Moses and direct his speech; and
Moses went.[3] There is all this evidence, and more, for the
biblical view that the prophet regarded himself as a passive instrument by whom—one might almost say "by
which"—God spoke.

But the evidence is not all in. The element of passivity,
acquiescence, surrender, in the prophetic experience of
men having the stature of Amos, Isaiah, Jeremiah, and
Ezekiel must contend with another. This other element,
the hesitant awe, the reluctance born of presumed inade-
quacy, first appears before the prophet ever accepts his
prophetic role. It seems almost to be a necessary feature
of the prophetic call. God must overcome the man's reserve
before he can own him and send him and speak through
him. It has just been noted that Moses demurred: "Who
am I to go to Pharaoh?" and "I am not a man of words"
and he had to be convinced. The searing coal was brought
to the lips of Isaiah only after he had cried in dismay:
"I am a man of unclean lips." [4] Like Solomon who, when
he was called to kingship, protested that he was a mere
child and whom God comforted in his dream,[5] and like
Gideon who, when called to military leadership, pleaded
incompetency, being of the poorest family of Menasseh
and himself the least of his household, and whom then
God promised to stand by [6]—like them, Jeremiah, when
he was called to assume the mantle of prophecy, wonder-
ing exclaimed: "Alas, Lord God! I know not how to speak,
being a mere lad" (1:6). But God overcame his original
hesitancy as he had overcome that of Moses and Isaiah
and the others, and Jeremiah became a prophet.

[3] Exod. 4:10-12.   [5] I Kings 3:5-15.
[4] Isa. 6:5-7.   [6] Judg. 6:15 f.

There is no good reason to doubt that chapter 1 contains Jeremiah's initial prophetic experience. The account there is prefaced with a three-verse "title page" and interrupted (in vv. 11 to 12 and 13 to 16) by two brief accounts of later visions, so that Jeremiah's own narrative of his call is limited to vv. 4 to 10 and 17 to 19. But it is there, and it is probably a faithful account, by and large, of what as a young man the prophet experienced. Nevertheless one may legitimately ask when in his life the prophet recorded for "publication" this early experience. Was it at once? Or did some years of living intervene—time for him to learn of the hazards of his occupation and the limits which men set for a prophet's accomplishment? A lapse of years between the call and the record of the call is indeed probable. There is too much anticipation of difficulty, too much cognizance here of the possibility of failure. Lacking discouraging experiences, are not young men more sanguine? Do they need the repeated assurances? "Do not fear . . . I am with you . . . to save you. . . . Gird up your loins . . . Do not be discouraged by them . . . If they fight with you they will not succeed . . . I am with you . . . to save you."

If it seems plausible that Jeremiah committed his vision to writing only after adversity had revealed to him the true dimensions of his undertaking on God's behalf, the question next arises: Why and at what later time did he thus set forth the circumstances of his call? Why and for whom did he suppose that the record held interest? An answer is possible. Consider what it is that the prophet really says in his account, what information he intends to convey, what point he makes. It is simply this: that God authorized him to speak, putting words in his mouth. It is as though his right had been challenged and he

needed to defend it. So he produces his charter, certifica-
tion, diploma. This, he says, is how it happened and why
I speak in God's name; "God said to me . . . : Wherever
I send you you shall go . . . whatever I command you
you shall speak . . . I am with you . . . He put forth
his hand and touched my mouth . . . God said to me:
Lo, I have put my words in your mouth . . . I am with
you." The record here of Jeremiah's call is a document
attesting to his right to speak for God.

There was more than one occasion in his life when
Jeremiah had to defend his right to speak in God's name,
and any one of them could have evoked his statement,
for the record. Certainly, for example, this statement of
his would have had meaning at the time of his trial, when
indeed the one point that he made in his own defense
was this: that God had sent him. "It was God who sent
me to prophesy . . . all of the words which you have
heard. . . . Truly God sent me to speak to you all of
these words" (26:12-15).[7] The time of his trial "early in
the reign of Jehoiakim" (26:1) is quite conceivably though
not necessarily the time when Jeremiah both clutched at
the memory and put into words for all times the experience of a score of years before, in Josiah's "thirteenth year"
(1:2); it was probably then that he wrote his deposition.

It is a deposition and not a diploma. There was no one
to sign it and affix a seal other than Jeremiah himself. No
other than he could attest to his unshared experience of
God. He knew what he knew, of course. At his trial he
could say, "It was God who sent me . . . truly God sent
me," but he could bring no proof, produce no witnesses.
He knew because it had happened. He could, as in his
first chapter he does, circumstantially describe the man-

[7] See above, pp. 16 f.

ner of God's sending. He could say, "He put forth his hand and touched my mouth." But he could do no more than say it.

This is the form of his narrative, the first of the documents of self-revelation in his book:

I received the word of God:
> Before I shaped you in the womb I knew you;
> Before you went from the womb I adopted you;
> I designated you a prophet . . .[8]

And I said:
> Alas, Lord God! I know not how to speak
> Being a mere lad.

And God said to me:
> Do not say: "I am a lad";
> For, wherever I send you you shall go,
> And whatever I command you you shall speak.
> Do not fear . . .
> For I am with you, God says, to save you.

And God put forth his hand and touched my mouth.
And God said to me:
> Lo, I have put my words in your mouth.
> See, I have designated you today [a prophet] . . .[9]
> To root out and tear down,
> And to lay waste and destroy,
> To rebuild and to replant.

> . . . Now you gird up your loins;
> Get up and say to them
> All that I charge you.
> Do not be discouraged by them
> Or I will break you before them.
> But I, lo, I make you this day as a fortified city,

[8] See Fourth Additional Note, p. 242.
[9] *Idem.*

> As an iron pillar, and as walls of bronze
> Over against the whole land,
> The kings of Judah and her princes,
> Her priests and the people of the land.
> If they fight with you they will not succeed,
> For I am with you, God says, to save you (1:4-10, 17-19).

A second document which, though without affixed date of composition, probably refers to an early period in the life of the prophet, appears in chapter 16:1-9. The reason for the conjecture that it refers to his earlier years, those years between his call and the trial, the years in Josiah's reign when Jeremiah had not yet reached the age of forty, is the fact that he here explains why he has not married and had children. This is no compelling argument for a date, and he could as well have phrased his explanation near the end of his life. Actually there is this notable difference between the biographical sections and the documents of self-revelation in his book, that though the former are normally dated, the latter are undated and the clues to their times and the occasions to which they severally refer are almost totally lacking. For what it is worth, one observes that the passage in chapter 16, at least refers to the time in Jeremiah's life when he might have been expected to marry and have children. This is what he says of his bachelorhood:

> I received this word of God:
> You shall neither marry nor have sons or daughters in this place; for so God has said of the sons and daughters that are born in this place and of their mothers that bear and their fathers that beget them in this land: they will die diseased; they will not be lamented or buried; they will lie

as offal on the ground. They will be consumed by sword and famine, and their dead bodies will be food for the fowl of heaven and the beasts of earth (16:1-4).

Whether or not the statement is taken at face value, that is to say whether he meant "word of God" to include the whole statement or recognized a part of it as his personal contribution, two facts at any rate emerge: that Jeremiah was not a married man with family, and that he expected a horrible end for the people of his land. Jeremiah connected the two facts in his statement: it was immoral to bring children to life in a doomed society and therefore he had not married. Hebrew prophets did not practice celibacy; Hosea, Isaiah, and Ezekiel mention their wives, Samuel had sons, as did other unnamed prophets.[10] Jeremiah here records the fact that he is unmarried by design. It would have taken a strong woman to share the stress and sorrow of his life, but his pain was without doubt greater because he had no family for comfort.

Jeremiah explains in this same composition why he was avoiding people and not joining them in their times of grief or pleasure:

For so God said:
Neither enter a banquet house nor join in mourning, and do not condole with them, for I have withdrawn my peace from this people, God says, the devotion and compassion. And great and small will die in this land and lie unburied; none will lament for them, none will gash himself or shave the head for them. None will provide [bread for the be-

[10] See Hos. 1:2; Isa. 8:3; Ezek. 24:18; I Sam. 12:2; I Kings 13:11; II Kings 4:1.

reaved] to comfort him for his loss, and they will not offer
[him] the cup of consolation for father or for mother.

And do not enter a house of feasting to sit with them to
eat or drink. For so said the Lord of hosts, the God of
Israel: In this place, before your eyes and in your days I
will put an end to

> the voice of joy,
> the voice of rejoicing,
> the voice of the bridegroom,
> the voice of the bride (16:5-9).

Again two facts emerge: Jeremiah led a life withdrawn,
and (again) he believed his people doomed. He connected
these two facts also: because God had withdrawn his
peace from his people, therefore his prophet was to keep
himself apart.

It is hard to avoid the impression upon reading Jeremiah's statement in this sixteenth chapter that the prophet
wrote it in anger and in desperation. He sounds almost
as though he wished these horrors to overtake the people.
That is by no means the general tone of his ministry
—it is contrary to the general tone of his ministry—
but the misanthropic mood is not lacking in this composition.

For the pattern of Jeremiah's life the passage suggests
that he was stalked by loneliness. Other bits of evidence
agree. In the midst of a prayer he exclaims with some
bitterness:

> I sat not in the company of merrymakers
> Exulting in the joy of my heart.
> I sat alone because of your irresistible power,
> For you filled me with gloom (15:17 with two words from
>   v. 16).

In an outburst of loathing he rejects his kinsmen:

> Oh that I had a lodge in the wilderness
> That I might leave my people and go from them,
> For they are all adulterers, a troop of liars! (9:1)

In an apostrophe to his mother he at once confesses and bemoans his state of alienation:

> Woe unto me, my mother, that you bore me
> A man of strife and contention on all sides!
> I have been neither a lender nor a borrower
> Yet everyone curses me (15:10).

He addresses the same plaint to God:

> I have heard the calumny of the multitude . . .
> Even my [presumed] friends
> Watch for me to slip (20:10).

And he makes God the source of the suspicions which he harbors and his mistrust of persons near him. God seems to have told him:

> Even your brothers, those of your own household,
> Even they have deceived you;
> Even they have loudly declaimed against you.
> Trust them not though they speak of you amiably (12:6).

His "brothers," his "household," are the people of Anathoth. Jeremiah was "the son of Hilkiyahu among the priests who were in Anathoth in the land of Benjamin" (1:1). It was from Anathoth his kinsman came offering a field for sale (32:7 f.), and Jeremiah, when he was arrested, was bound for Benjamin to take possession there

of an ancestral field (37:12). So it is they whom he mis-
trusts, his family in Anathoth, and apparently with good
reason. He has heard God refer to them as "the people of
Anathoth who seek your life and say: 'You shall not
prophesy in God's name lest you die by our hands'"
(11:21).

Without wife or children, suspicious of his own brothers
and kinsmen, believing his "friends" to be treacherous,
at odds with most men and ready to renounce their society, he was a homeless, lonely man. That he should give
vent to his torment as he does in one of the most poignant
documents of self-revelation in our literature is no surprise.
It is found at the end of the twentieth chapter (vv. 14-18).
It is an undirected cry, a blast of unreasoned anger. It
has the form of a curse yielding to a rhetorical question, a
querulous "Why?"—but more a whimper than a question.
Jeremiah curses the day on which he was born and he
curses the man who spread news of his birth; he details
his curse upon the man and he gives the avowed reason
for his curses, seeking so to justify his wrath. And then
he asks a question which he wants no one to answer.

> Accursed be the day on which I was born;
> Let the day my mother bore me not be blessed.
> Accursed be the man who informed my father, saying:
> "A male child has been born to you," making him very glad;
> And let that man be as the cities which God overthrew
>   without mercy,
> And let him hear a shriek in the morning, a battle cry at
>   noon-tide,
> Because I did not die at the time of birth,
> My mother serving as my grave, her womb ever great with
>   me.
> Why, indeed, did I come from the womb

To experience trouble and grief and to waste my days in
   shame? (20:14-18)

The symbols are fairly clear; the lodge in the wilderness,
the grave, the womb, are to Jeremiah a refuge, warmth
and peace ("caldo nell' eterna pace"), escape from un-
welcome responsibility. Jeremiah wants to run away,
brings aversion to his task, does not now relish his mission.
His distaste borders on the urge toward extinction. That is
why he curses the day and the man, quite irrationally
makes scapegoats of a measure of time and a well-meaning
friend of the family. And his curse in the twentieth chapter combines with Jeremiah's statement in the sixteenth
to account for his loneliness. He shunned the society which
rejected him.

But he also loved his people. And if this be ambivalence
we have to make the best of it.

VI

What Jeremiah Held Back

When the relation between prophet and God is more thoroughly explored, an element other than resignation appears—an element in tension with the prophet's surrender of self. A prophet characteristically holds something in reserve, is not wholly possessed by his God, remains a self in communication with God, the other self. And this self of the prophet can personally love the people which, as God's prophet, at God's bidding he condemns. It was notably so with Jeremiah, in whom the strain seemed more than he could bear. For Jeremiah had more than his share of the love for his people which warred with his calling as messenger of doom.

Other prophets experienced the conflict which Jeremiah knew. Amos and Ezekiel, Micah and Isaiah met with his experience, but none suffered as Jeremiah did because of it. Hosea, though he is popularly known as "the prophet of love," gives less evidence than these others do of resistance to the message he brings, less reserve over against God; but this may be because chance here preserved so little that is autobiographical. It is hazardous to suggest that Hosea took issue with God when he addressed to him this one sudden word of prayer:

Give them, O Lord—what shall you give them?
Give them a miscarrying womb and drying breasts
  (Hos. 9:14).

That this cruel word conceals compassion, being merely a request that infants mercifully die rather than live for suffering, is improbable. The prophet could as well be supplementing God's threat as seeking to soften it. And in the one longer first-person document in Hosea (the third chapter) the prophet conceives the ratio: As Hosea is to his wife, God is to his people, and leaves no room for a special liaison between prophet and people. For want of evidence to the contrary, then, Hosea appears as a prophet who identified with God withholding nothing.

It is different with Amos and Ezekiel, Micah and Isaiah —and certainly with Jeremiah.

Amos recorded five visions, two of which have a particular interest here. In those two, seeing calamity sweep across the land, a caterpillar plague, a conflagration, Amos prayed. "Ah, Lord God: Forgive!" he asked, and again: "Ah, Lord God! Desist! How can Jacob stand, being small?" (Amos 7:2, 5). A surprising note of tenderness, this intercession in one whose message otherwise is wholly stern and uncompromising. With these visions of Amos in mind, George Adam Smith [1] was prompted to say: "Never to a people came there a true prophet who had not first prayed for them." If not even Amos could coldly condemn and repeat without remonstrance the divinely planted

[1] *The Book of the Twelve Prophets . . . I, The Expositor's Bible* (New York: G. H. Doran Co., 1912[?]), p. 113.

word, then the prophet who could do so must be rare.
Ezekiel, too, normally pliant and the passive instrument of
God's revelation, had on two occasions to shrink back in
dismay and intervene with God.

> I was left alone and I fell on my face and cried:
> "Ah, Lord God! Are you destroying the remnant of Israel,
> Spilling your wrath on Jerusalem?" (Ezek. 9:8)

And again:

> I fell on my face and cried aloud: "Ah, Lord God!
> Are you finishing off the remnant of Israel?" (Ezek. 11:13)

So neither of these prophets, not Amos nor Ezekiel, was
that absorbed in God that he and God were one mind, one
voice. These prophets spoke for God, but they likewise
spoke to God, and almost, it may be said, they called him
to account.

Micah voiced his alarm:

> . . . I lament and I wail,
> Go barefoot and unclothed,
> Like the jackals make lamentation,
> Make mourning like ostriches,
> For grievous is her blow,
> For it has come unto Judah,
> Has reached the gate of my people,
> Even Jerusalem (Mic. 1:8 f.).

The point is that here the prophet is speaking. Though
he serves as God's mouth he can yet stand off and express
his dismay at what God has wrought.

Isaiah was no more vulnerable than Amos. He too had

a thick skin and could reprove and admonish and speak to his people of a total and final disaster. Yet there was a crack in his armor and in two places in particular it appears. Once, in the consecration vision, not where, in keeping with the style of such visions,[2] he hesitates, but at a later stage after God has overcome the man's doubts, as with all prophets God had to do, and after Isaiah has then offered himself: "I am ready; send me then," and God has said: "Go, and speak," and has revealed to him the nature of his work—after all of this, still with three words the prophet's self asserts itself and his dismay bursts from him: "Lord, how long?" (Isa. 6:11). He is not here asking whether it is a two-year contract; we are acquainted with this cry. It is common in the Psalms where an agonized "eternally" is often joined to it: "How long! . . . How eternally long!"[3]

And one prophetic word besides, suggests that Isaiah's compelling message was a source of grief to him personally. That word occurs in what may have been the last of his utterances, spoken after the Assyrian Sennacherib broke camp and left for home. Isaiah did not then join the jubilant throng madly celebrating the sudden relief. Still he saw chariotry and horsemen about the walls, still heard the cry of war at the gates; tragedy still lurked in the valley of his vision. The scene visible to his inner eye and yet to be realized, wrung from him this second agonized cry:

> "Avert your eyes; let me weep bitterly.
> Seek not to console me for the tragedy of the daughter of
>   my people" (Isa. 22:4).

[2] See above, pp. 70 f.
[3] See Ps. 13:2; 74:10; 79:5; 89:47; similarly Ps. 85:6; 90:13; Hab. 1:2.

This Isaiah was not here acting out a part; Ezekiel did
that at times [4] but not Isaiah. Nor was he weeping out of
chagrin, as well he might have done since overnight he
had been discredited. This was not chagrin but true affliction. Jeremiah in his tenderest moments was to use the
same language later. Isaiah's expression "daughter of my
people" is at home in elegies; Jeremiah used it when he
lamented the battered nation.[5] And this same prophet
echoed Isaiah's other phrase. Isaiah said: "Let me weep
bitterly"; and using the same Hebrew terms Jeremiah
referred to Rachel's weeping for her children:

> Hark! Lamentation is heard in Ramah,
> Bitter weeping,
> Rachel weeping for her children, inconsolable—
> For her children, because they are not (31:15).

There can be no doubt that these words of Isaiah were
the expression of genuine grief. And if with this desperate
cry we couple his anguished question "Lord, how long?"
we have, to be sure, not a great abundance but nevertheless some quite convincing evidence of tenderness in
Isaiah, a tenderness which, as a "man of principle," he
appears rather successfully to have submerged, sat upon,
suppressed, lest it deflect him even for a moment from
his prophetic course. This discipline was necessary because in a sense his tenderness was a personal heresy. It
was his protest, his reservation, that part of himself which
he did not surrender when he accepted the prophetic call.

These observations lead on to Jeremiah, the prophet in
whom the tension between surrender of self and assertion
of self was the most violent. Amos, Isaiah, Ezekiel—even
though with a fanatic abandon they served their master—

---

[4] E.g., in Ezek. 21:11 f.
[5] See especially Jer. 8:18-23, below, pp. 86 f.

were not absorbed in him as in mystic union. They still could stand aside and listen to their own tragic words and view the breaking of the daughter of their people, and themselves experience affliction. They could pray; they could protest. But none of them was nearly as articulate about the inner stress as Jeremiah. No one so openly expressed his private grief; no prophet left so faithful a record of his prayers.

Like Amos and Ezekiel, Jeremiah prayed for his people. When Jeremiah was Jeremiah and not God's agent he interceded with God for his people. When he spoke not for God but to God in prayer he prayed for them. Though forbidden—

Pray not for good for this people . . . (14:11),

Do not pray for this people,
Or take up for them any cry or prayer,
Or intercede with me,
For I will not hear you (7:16)

—though thus twice forbidden, he yet dared to pray. And he even admitted his insubordination in a word addressed to God—yes, claimed it as a virtue:

Is good to be rewarded with evil? . . .
Remember how I stood before you,
To speak good on their behalf,
To avert your anger from them (18:20).

He spoke of it twice:

. . . Indeed I interceded with you in a time of calamity
And in a time of distress on behalf of the enemy [6] (15:11).

[6] Grimly, "the enemy" here, as in Isa. 1:24, is God's people, Israel.

And it became a matter of record that once the king and once the people sought him out to pray for them,[7] which they would hardly have done had their errand seemed implausible.

There is one passage in which the prophet appears to have recognized the ambiguity of his position. There, again in a word addressed to God, he says:

> I have neither sought to escape serving you
> Nor desired the grievous day (17:16).

Serving God he had announced, but being Jeremiah he had not desired "the grievous day."

Jeremiah would of course pray for his people. He loved the people and with obvious grief contemplated the suffering which was their destiny. "Would my head were water," he lamented, "and my eyes a spring of tears!" His elegy is found at the end of the eighth chapter. He imagines his people already in exile:

> . . . Grief overwhelms me.[8] I am sick at heart.
> Lo, the sound of the cry of the daughter of my people
> From a distant land:
> "Is God not in Zion?
> Is her king not there? . . .
> The harvest time is over, the summer is done,
> And we are not delivered."
> I am utterly broken in the breaking of the daughter of my
>   people;
> I am sunk in gloom, desolation has seized me.
> Is there no balm in Gilead?
> Is no physician there?
> Why has there not been found

[7] Jer. 21:2; 42:2.
[8] Reading 'alah for 'ale.

> Healing for the daughter of my people?
> Would my head were water
> And my eyes a spring of tears!
> I would weep day and night
> For the slain of the daughter of my people (8:18-23).

Jeremiah could not simply accept the fate of his people as something divinely done and therefore good. And he did not withhold his grief, the overflow of his protest.

In a similar passage in the thirteenth chapter he links with his plea the prospect of his grief if his people reject the plea:

> Hearken and hear! Be not proud,
> For God has spoken.
> Honor the Lord your God
> Before night falls,
> Before your feet blunder
> Over mountains of dusk
> And you hope for light but he blacks it out
> [And turns it] to darkness.
> Yet, if you will not hearken
> I must privately weep
> For the arrogance—and shed tears
> And my eyes drop tears
> That God's flock is in captivity (13:15-17).

If the people reject his plea, if they will not hearken, he must weep at the fate which their arrogant refusal will inevitably entail.

It is not surprising that tradition attributed to Jeremiah the authorship of the five laments which make up the biblical book of Lamentations. Though he did not write that book Jeremiah possessed such natural tenderness and could so well put up his feelings in words that he was

master of the dirge and his laments are unexcelled. His
book contains other elegies. A longer elegy marked by
feeling and skill begins in v. 9 of chapter 9 and is resumed
in vv. 16-21. Whether here the ruin he describes is present
and actual or envisioned in prospect, it is real for the
prophet and he must weep with the victims as he con-
templates the scene.

ce. 9:16-21   I take up a cry and a lament for the mountains,
        Lamentation for the wilderness pastures,
        That they are ruined with none passing through
        And hear no sound of cattle.
        The fowl of the air and the beasts—
        They have departed, they are gone.

        . . . Summon wailing women; let them come.
        Send for wise women; let them come quickly
        And take up for us a lament.
        Let our eyes [too] drop tears,
        Our eyelids stream.
        For, hear! Lament is heard in Zion:
        "How are we ruined! How greatly disgraced!
        For we must leave the land,
        For they have discarded [?] our dwellings."
        Yes, hear, you women, the word of God;
        Apprehend the word of his mouth
        And teach your daughters a lament,
        Each the other a lamentation;
        For death came in at our windows,
        Entered our citadels,
        Cutting down children without,
        Youths in the streets.
        . . . And human corpses lie around
        Like dung in fields,
        Like sheaves behind the reaper,
        With none to collect them.

If possible, the dirge in chapter 14 surpasses even this one in intensity. It seems to have been spoken in a time of drought and universal distress; and here the prophet's understanding encompasses the creatures of the wild along with humankind.

Judah mourns,
Her gates languish;
They look darkly at the ground,
The cry of Jerusalem ascends.
Her lords sent their lads out for water;
They came to the cisterns,
They did not find water.
They returned with vessels empty.
The farmers are broken because of the ground;
Because there has been no rain in the land
They are shamed and abashed and cover the head.[9]
Yes, even the doe in the open field calves
    and abandons [her young]
For there is no grass.
Wild asses stand on bare heights,
Snuff wind like jackals,
With glazed eyes, for there is no pasture (14:2-6).

There is more here than the eye of an alert witness, a reporter carefully recording observed details. There is a sympathy that penetrates beneath the surface of things seen. The prophet has himself become the lords of Jerusalem, the abashed farmer, the doe and wild ass. His sensibility is such that he partakes of what he describes. Sensitive and tender he takes the grief to himself and it is his own. And so it is that later in this same chapter, in what is probably an extension of this same lament (though sword and famine have replaced the drought as the occa-

---

[9] The Hebrew text here has the words in a different order and contains some repetition.

sion for Jerusalem's grief), he mourns as one who himself
is bereaved:

> . . . Let my eyes descend in tears
> And not cease night or day,
> For broken with an awful breaking
> Is the virgin, the daughter of my people—
> A most grievous blow.
> If I go out to the open field
> Ah, those slain by the sword!
> If I enter the city
> Ah, those perishing of hunger! (14:17-18)

This extension of the lament makes explicit what was already implied, that Jeremiah's description of the suffering
was not that of a detached spectator but of one who himself suffered with the people he loved.

There is another passage which leads to the same conclusion. Here, into a public lament Jeremiah dramatically
interpolates an expression of his own feelings. He is repeating a dirge which he has put in the mouth of Jerusalem, when he suddenly interrupts the presumed words
of the personified city with his own uncontrollable grief.
The emphatic first person pronoun "myself" signifies the
change in speaker.[10] Only the line so introduced (here in
parentheses) is his own; the rest is Jerusalem's dirge.

> Alas! I am crushed; grievous the blow!
> (Myself, I said: "This is affliction indeed, and I bear it.")
> My tent is down,
> All its ropes are torn loose.
> My children have left me and are no more;
> None is there to stretch my curtains,
> To raise again my tent [11] (10:19 f.).

[10] Compare the similarly emphatic use of the pronoun in Micah 3:8.
[11] The Hebrew text has the words for "curtains" and "tent" transposed.

Into the lamenting chorus Jeremiah flings his own lament: "This is affliction indeed, and I bear it," or, if several ancient translations have read the text right, with one of the letters doubled: [12] "This is indeed *my* affliction, and I bear it." The prophet is no disinterested bystander, observer, spectator. He is borne along in the tragedy, involved in the general grief. On his own part the prophet laments.

It is so, then: Jeremiah would of course pray for his people, must pray because he loved his people and their suffering was his suffering. Though restrained by his God the prophet would assert his identity and dissuade God, if he could, in order that the people might endure.

Jeremiah may seem to be betraying his God. He is indeed making himself out the more tender, the one more concerned for the people's welfare. In one of the two passages already cited where God forbids Jeremiah to pray,[13] God is unyielding and determined as against a prophet who might hope to sway him in favor of a suppliant people.

And God said to me:
Pray not for good for this people.
If they fast I will not listen to their cries.
If they bring me sacrifice and offering I
    will not favor them
For I will consume them with sword and hunger
    and disease (14:11 f.).

But if here God appears less "human" than his prophet— if Jeremiah's God appears merely stern, this is not his only visage, as other evidence suggests.

[12] The Targum, the Vulgate, Aquila, and Symmachus appear to have read *hlyy*.
[13] See above, p. 85.

VII

How Jeremiah Prayed for His People

The more one looks into the matter the more complicated it appears. The first chapter of Jeremiah's book, the narrative of his call, his surrender, is only a beginning. There is not only that initial hesitancy: "I am a lad" (1:6), which God overcomes with a touch of a finger, but there is a lifetime of willingness to serve his master, and of unwillingness—a willingness made difficult by the prophet's love for his people and an unwillingness moderated by his loyalty to God. Because he was loyal to God and to his own prophetic office Jeremiah admonished and scourged a calloused people. But because he loved this people he prayed for them at the same time. With the God whom he obeyed he remonstrated. And in his prayers the ambiguity is unmistakable. In Jeremiah's prayers all of the complex lines of his relationship with his people and his God come together in a tangled skein.

Incidentally, Jeremiah is the only prophet whose prayers are on record in a sufficient quantity to invite analysis. They are all but unique in prophetic literature.

Jeremiah prayed both for himself and for his people. What he said when he prayed for himself is more easily assembled than what he said when he prayed on behalf of others. Indeed, six magnificent prayer compositions within the biblical book of Jeremiah contain words which he addressed to God out of the perplexities of his own heart, and the study of them is rewarding. But when, prior to an analysis in Chapter VIII of these extended prayers on his own behalf, we undertake here to survey Jeremiah's intercessory activity for others, we find the material less readily available. The record contains suggestions of such activity, to be sure, but there is disappointingly little in the way of actual quotations from his prayers of this sort. Here, except for one composition a few lines long, we are left with mere traces of prayer, a word or a phrase.

That Jeremiah did pray on behalf of his people is apparent from evidence already surveyed. There are four good reasons for believing that he did:

(1) The king and the people asked him to pray for them quite as though this were a natural request—quite as though the prophet had done so on other occasions. Zedekiah sent to him saying:

"Apply [derash-na'] to God on our behalf, since Nebuchadrezzar king of Babylon is making war on us. Perhaps God will act for us according to all his wonders and [Nebuchadrezzar] will go from us" (21:2).

Similarly, after Gedaliah's murder the refugees from Judah said to him:

"Let our petition sway you, and pray [hithpallel] to the Lord your God on our behalf for all this remnant, for we remain few out of many as you see us; so may the Lord your God tell us of the way we should go and what we should do" (42:2-3).

Both king and people spoke as though they knew that
Jeremiah would not refuse them.

(2) In view of his love for his people and the grief
with which he contemplated their fate (reviewed in the
foregoing chapter),[1] Jeremiah would be inclined to intercede for his people and to remonstrate with God in order
to avert their doom, if so he might. The man who must
say: "I am utterly broken in the breaking of the daughter
of my people," "This is affliction indeed, and I bear it,"
"If you will not hearken I must privately weep for the arro-
gance—and shed tears . . . that God's flock is in captivity," "Would my head were water and my eyes a spring
of tears!" "Broken with an awful breaking is the virgin,
the daughter of my people"—the man so loving, who must
so plaintively lament, must also pray.

(3) Jeremiah records the repeated divine prohibition,[2]
evidence that both he and his God were aware of this
prophet's disposition to pray. If Jeremiah has refrained
from praying for his people, he implies, or if he has prayed
but seldom—for he has prayed—that is because God had
restrained him. He had been charged: "Pray not for good
for this people." And again: "Do not pray for this people . . . or intercede with me." The very fact that he is
cautioned not to pray betrays his predilection.

(4) Finally, he admits that though cautioned he has
prayed.[3] In a prayer of his own he reminds God of it:
Remember how I spoke "good on their behalf, to avert
your anger from them" and "I interceded with you in a
time of calamity." This fourth reason is the best. It is Jeremiah's own testimony—he prayed for his people.

It is clear then that he did so, however few of the words

[1] See above, pp. 86-91.
[2] See above, p. 85.
[3] See above, p. 85.

of such prayers are preserved, and with the little evidence at hand we can yet form an idea of the manner and content of his prayer. The few suggestions available contain intimations that although his prophetic message to his people was of their rejection, he prayed for reconciliation.

There are two sources of information on the nature and contents of Jeremiah's prayers for his people: the terminology for praying, which Jeremiah and his biographer employ, and the fragments of prayer which they include. First as to the terminology. The preferred terms were forms of the verbs *paga'* and *palal*, and the prayers would be prayers congenial to such terms. The Hebrew verb *paga'* means "to intercede." The verb *palal* means generally "to pray" but it has overtones of argument, of speech in defense of oneself or another, of pleading in a court of law. A third term which Jeremiah employs is the idiom "to stand before." This term is at home not in a court of law but in a royal court. It means "to wait upon" in the sense of using one's influence with the authorities. This last is the term which Jeremiah employs when he reminds God of his efforts for his people's good: "Remember how I stood before you to speak good on their behalf, to avert your anger from them" (18:20). And it is the term which God employs when he dissuades Jeremiah from any such efforts, suggesting that even greater prophets of earlier days, successful advocates then, could not influence him now in favor of his unresponsive people:

> And God said to me: "If Moses and Samuel stood before me I would not regard this people. Dismiss them. Let them leave" (15:1).

(Other biblical examples of the use of *paga'* and *palal* for prayer and an explanation of the interpretation proposed for the forms of *palal* are offered in the Second Additional Note, pp. 234-39.) Judged alone by his terminology for prayer, Jeremiah was a defender of his people, intervening, pleading, interceding for them with God—this despite the fact that he was sent to denounce and warn this people.

The second source of information on Jeremiah's prayers for his people is the language of the prayers themselves. The material is elusive. One has to supplement with inference the little evidence supplied by his one preserved prayer of this nature.

Jeremiah's response to Hananiah in 28:6 is the one extant composition which can be called a prayer in his own words for his people Israel. It was spoken at the beginning of his altercation with the "false" Hananiah.[4] That "prophet" had just said in God's name:

> . . . I have broken the yoke of Babylon's king. In another two years I will bring back to this place all the vessels of the Lord's house . . . and Jeconiah . . . and all the captivity of Judah . . . (28:2-4).

Jeremiah had heard Hananiah, and his response is his one such prayer. Perhaps he sighed as he spoke it and perhaps the people gasped when they heard him. For he asked what he knew could not be—though he wished it— and he said what the people believed him then incapable of saying. He was surely not speaking as prophet for God but as Jeremiah impulsively to God when, in response to Hananiah's words, he breathed his fervid "Amen!":

> "Amen! So may God do! Let God but fulfill the words of your prophecy and bring back from Babylonia to this place the vessels from God's house, and all the exiles . . ." (28:6).

[4] See above, pp. 39 f.

That is the total prayer and Jeremiah has left us the words of no others among the prayers which he prayed for his people.

But this one is clear enough. As for its form, there is nothing conventional about it. It is topical; it picks up the thought which is in everyone's mind and which Hananiah has just expressed. Here Jeremiah rephrases Hananiah's prediction, giving it the sound of a prayer, employing the modal form of the verbs: "So may God do! Let him but fulfill the words. . . ." As one often does in prayer, he addresses God in the third person, obliquely, asking this favor for his captive people: the restoration of the treasures from the looted temple, the return of the exiles of 598.

(Of incidental interest is the use of the word "amen," which word, like "hallelujah," has come into the English language directly from the Hebrew Bible. Its meaning is nowhere more readily apparent than here. It is defined by the immediately following exclamation: "So may God do!" It is a very solemn word, one probably at first connected with the taking of an oath. It is discussed more fully in the Third Additional Note, pp. 239-41.)

But it is the content, not the form, of this prayer that reveals Jeremiah's dilemma. Here in an unguarded moment his deeper feelings surface and betray him, and his mouth says what his heart desires—that Hananiah may be right and the captives will return, that, in other words, the worst may now be over. His wish was a personal heresy and he curbed it without delay. Nevertheless this one prayer remains. It is an instructive example of the prophet's prayers for the people; in form and content it probably resembles the unrecorded prayers of intervention and intercession to which he several times refers.[5]

[5] See above, pp. 93-95.

For want of further quotations from such prayers one turns to tangential evidence. A consideration of the terms which describe his prayer activity has already yielded a measure of understanding. A second indirect source is the occasional phrases or ejaculatory prayers which the prophet—himself their author—thinks into the mouths of others. Frequently within his book these seeds of prayer occur, and because in fact Jeremiah has composed them, they are in a sense his prayers for his people. They are the prayers he wished his people would pray. They are, as will appear, exclamations expressing submissive loyalty to God.

Consider first for contrast some examples of "un-prayer" in Jeremiah. For, not all speech addressed to God is prayer, and Jeremiah can quote rebellious words, petulant retorts, the impudent voicing of defiance and disloyalty, apparently current among the insensitive masses in his day. The reverse of prayer, these ejaculations are the imagined sullen replies of the people to a divine appeal.

I spoke to you in your languid ease;
You said: "I will not listen" (22:21).

And you said: "I will not serve [you]" (2:20).

So God said:
Stand by the ways and observe,
Ask of the ancient paths
Which way [leads to] good and follow it,
And find your security.
And they said: "We will not go."
And let me appoint watchmen for you;
[And] hearken to the alarm!
And they said: "We will not hearken" (6:16-17).

Have I been a wilderness to Israel,
Or a land of deep darkness? [God asks,]
Why have my people said: "We go our way [?];
We will not come back to you?" (2:31)

Do not run yourself barefoot
And parch your throat [God says].
But you said: "It is hopeless! No!
For I love strangers and will follow them" (2:25).

Smug denials supplement this defiance:

And you say: "But I am innocent;
Surely his anger will turn from me."
I will contend with you
Because you say: "I am not guilty" (2:35).

How can you say: "I am not soiled;
I did not go after the Baalim"? (2:23)

Confession here is wholly lacking: "I am not guilty,"
"I am not soiled; I did not go after the Baalim." There are
only the defiant refusals: "I will not listen," "I will not
serve [you]," "We will not go [on the way that leads to
good]," "We will not hearken," "It is hopeless! No!" "We
go our way; we will not come back to you."

But as against this rebellious mood, this negation of
prayer, Jeremiah wishfully imagined a different response,
one acceptable to God and meritorious. The prayers that
Jeremiah wished that his people had prayed in place of
their impudent denials—prayers of pious submission,
equally brief—occur as well. It is valid to draw from them
inferences as to the unrecorded prayers which he himself
prayed when, as he confessed, he prayed on his people's

behalf, and it is profitable to survey this material as it appears here and there in the midst of longer compositions.

Some of these short prayers are expressions of lack and need. They are phrased as questions and addressed obliquely to God, in the third person. "Where is God?," though a question, has the nature of prayer. Through his prophet God blames people, priest, prophet and "shepherd" (i.e., king) for the indifference which holds them back from asking "Where is God?"

> What wrong did your fathers find in me
> That they abandoned me
> To pursue without profit the profitless,
> And did not say: "Where is God
> Who took us from the land of Egypt,
> Who led us in the wilderness . . . ?"
> The priests did not say: "Where is God?"
> They that handle the law did not know me.
> The shepherds rebelled;
> The prophets prophesied for Baal,
> Pursued futilities (2:5-6, 8).

A question could also be an admission of guilt, the prelude to amendment.

> I have listened and heard;
> They do not speak right.
> No one deplores his wrongdoing
> And says: "[Alas!] What have I done?" (8:6).

Jeremiah implies that the asking of such questions (Where is God? What have I done?) would itself have been an act of devotion, an expression of lack and of need, and that the failure to ask was blameworthy.

Or not with questions but with a bare exclamation, the

people could have drawn near in prayer. Even a cry addressed to God could have been counted as prayer. If a people said only, "My father!" that would be prayer; it would signify loyalty—a second theme, along with lack and need. So Jeremiah spoke of God replacing threats with promises and showering gifts upon his people—doing so hopefully:

> I thought you would call me "My father!"
> And would not stray from me (3:19b).

The parallel "and would not stray from me" bears witness that the address "My father!" would have been a declaration of loyalty to God. It means: You are my father, as 3:4 demonstrates:

> Will you not now call me "My father!"
> [And say:] "You are the companion of my youth"?

The exclamation conveys the same meaning in 2:27, though there not God but idols of wood and stone are addressed as father and as mother ("wood" is masculine in Hebrew and "stone" is feminine):

> Saying to the wooden thing: "You are my father!"
> And to the one of stone: "You gave birth to me!"
> For to me [God is speaking] they turned the back
> And not the face;
> But in their time of distress they will say:
> "Arise and save us."

It is not to God but to the idols they have "turned the face" in that they said to them: "You are my father," "You gave birth to me." Their further prayer, "Arise and save us," would have had greater force, it is implied, if the earlier expression of loyalty had had God as its object. In 3:22b Jeremiah puts in the mouth of the people a declaration which though longer than "My father" means no more:

> "Here we are; we have come to you,
> For you are the Lord our God."

Perhaps this last declaration contains the sum of the matter and the clearest expression of the intent of all these ejaculatory prayers—except for one. Such cries as "My father!" and the like, or "You are the Lord our God!" mean merely this: "Here we are; we have come to you." If the questions express a feeling of guilt and a sense of need, the exclamations express a will towards reconciliation.

The one exception, the one cry with a slightly divergent intent among those which Jeremiah puts in the mouth of the people, is the one last cited above, the misdirected plea, "Arise and save us." In these short prayers this element of petition, the plea, is barely apparent—in the mouth of the people only here. It is, however, implicit in 27:18, where the "false" prophets are challenged:

> If they be prophets and have God's word, let them intercede with the Lord of Hosts that the vessels left in God's house and the house of Judah's king and in Jerusalem come not to Babylon.

Without wording the prayer, Jeremiah here names its mood and suggests its content. The prophets are to "intercede" (a form of Hebrew *paga‘*), asking that the city and its treasures be spared from Babylon's might. Jeremiah refers also in 36:7 to a prayer ("supplication," Heb.

tehinnah) of the people without specifying the words: "Perhaps their supplication will fall before God . . . for great is the anger and the wrath with which God has threatened his people." And in his letter to the exiles of 598 Jeremiah invites them to pray for the welfare of the city of their captivity (29:7) and to call upon God and to pray to him in the confidence that he will respond (29:12).[6] If we had the words of these imagined prayers, the intercession and the supplication, they would no doubt resemble the plea: "Arise and save us."

There is also one longer prayer which Jeremiah put in the mouth of the people, the people here being the survivors of the northern kingdom, Ephraim:

> I clearly heard Ephraim lamenting:
> "You chastened me and I was chastened,
> Being like an untrained calf.
> Take me back and I will return,
> For you are the Lord my God;
> For after I turned away I was sorry,
> And after I was given to know I smote my thigh,
> I was shamed and disgraced;
> Indeed I bore the reproach of my youth" (31:18-19).

This prayer contains two elements already familiar and one which is new. The words: "For you are the Lord my God" are identical, except for the singular pronoun, with 3:22 (". . . for you are the Lord our God") reviewed among the exclamatory prayers expressing loyalty. And the words "Take me back and I will return" are the element of petition or plea which appeared, though only once, in 2:27: "Arise and save us." Those are the familiar elements. The one new form is the narrative, the descrip-

[6] See Second Additional Note, p. 237.

tion which makes up the rest of the prayer, the restate-
ment of what happened and with what results: "You
chastened me and I was chastened . . . sorry . . . smote
my thigh . . . was shamed . . . disgraced . . . bore the
reproach of my youth." The narrative has purpose. God
chastened Ephraim—that is briefly told; but then the
repetitious detailing of the results—this telling is designed
to assure God that his chastening had been productive.
Now God can respond to the plea—can take Ephraim
back. The narrative form is new, but the mood has appeared before. It was the mood of the questions, "Where
is God?" and "What have I done?"

One final passage [7] seems to match the mood evident
here in this narrative description of Ephraim's disgrace.
It is now the concluding verse (v. 25) of Jer. 3, but once
it may have followed directly on v. 22 of that chapter.
If the two verses are read in sequence the will towards
reconciliation in the one is supported by contrition in
the other:

> "Here we are; we have come to you
> For you are the Lord our God . . .
> Let us lie down in our shame
> And be covered with disgrace . . ." (3:22, 25).

The cumulative evidence suggests that when Jeremiah
prayed for his people it was for this that he prayed: that
people and God become reconciled one to the other. This
he prayed out of love for the people whom at God's command he was impelled to condemn.

---

[7] Several other extended prayers in the book of Jeremiah are attributed
to the people, but since these appear to be compositions by later hands
they are not immediately relevant. For one of the most beautiful among
them (14:7-9, 19-22), see Fourth Additional Note, pp. 244 f.

VIII

How Jeremiah Prayed for Himself

As concerns himself Jeremiah asked for justice. He only wanted what was just and right. At least, so he thought; he found it all very confusing. As is usual in prayer, when Jeremiah prayed for himself he sought to influence his God toward a desired response. His prayer had the form of *tephillah*.[1] As a litigant spreads his case before a judge or jury, urging his own innocence, enlarging on the perfidy of his adversaries, asking for them destruction, for himself a favorable verdict, so Jeremiah appeared in prayer before God, his judge, to plead his desperate case.

Six passages document this description of Jeremiah's praying. In them all, as a man does in prayer, the prophet addresses God; in one of the six he moves on from prayer to meditation on God. A portion follows on four of the prayers which explicitly or by implication represents the divine response to the prophet's appeal. The six prayers occur within the second ten chapters of Jeremiah's book: at the end of chapter 11, at the beginning of chapter 12, and in chapters 15, 17, 18, and 20. The passages follow here in translation, though not in the biblical order. Instead, they are disposed in an order which suggests a cer-

[1] See Second Additional Note, pp. 236-39.

tain development in the prophet's thought. It would be hazardous to suppose that here the prayers are now arranged in the original chronological order, but the exposition should demonstrate that as they are here ordered there is some progress in thought from one to another. The verses are numbered for easier reference in the subsequent analysis, and the few departures from the received text are indicated in the footnotes.

FIRST PRAYER: 17:14-18

14 Heal me, O Lord, and I shall be healed;
  Save me, and I shall be saved—
  For you are the object of my praise.
15 Lo, they say to me:
  "Where is this word of God?
  Let it come to pass!"
16 Yet I have neither sought to escape serving you
  Nor desired the grievous day.
  You know what comes from my lips;
  It is ever before you.
17 Be not my ruin;
  You are my refuge in a day of distress.
18 Let them be ashamed that persecute me, but
    let me not be ashamed.
  Let them be dismayed, but let me not be dismayed.
  Bring on them the day of evil,
  And destroy them with a double destruction.

SECOND PRAYER: 18:18-23

Preface

18 They said: "Come, let us plot against Jeremiah,
  For teaching has not departed from the priest
  Nor counsel from the sage, nor the word from the
    prophet.

> Come, let us smite him on the tongue
> And hear no more of his words."

The Prayer

19 Give heed to me, O Lord,
And hearken to the voice of them that contend with me.
20 Is good to be rewarded with evil? . . .[2]
Remember how I have stood before you
To speak good on their behalf,
To avert your anger from them.
21 Therefore: deliver up their children to famine
And give them over to the power of the sword;
And let their women be bereft of children and widowed;
And let their men be slain,
Their young men smitten by the sword in battle.
22 Let a cry be heard from their houses
When you bring a troop suddenly on them—
For they have digged a pit to take me
And hid snares for my feet.
23 You know, O Lord,
That they plotted my death.
Forgive not their iniquity,
Nor blot out [3] their sin from your sight;
But let them be brought to stumble before you;
Deal with them in the time of your anger.

THIRD PRAYER: 11:18; 12:6; [4] 11:19-23

The Prayer

11:18 You informed me, O Lord,[5] and I perceived it.
You made me aware of their doings, [saying:]

---

[2] The clause here omitted is in place where it occurs a second time in verse 22.

[3] Reading the verb as a *ḳal* (second person masculine singular): *timaḥ*.

[4] As many have observed, this verse, which has no relation to its context in chapter 12, completes the thought of 11:18 and belongs here.

[5] Because otherwise in these prayers God is addressed "O Lord!" the

12:6 "Even your brothers, those of your own household,
Even they have deceived you;
Even they have loudly declaimed against you.
Trust them not though they speak of you amiably."

11:19 And I had been as a gentle lamb
Led to the slaughter,
Not aware that they were plotting against me:
"Let us destroy the tree in its sap; [6]
Let us cut him off from the land of the living
That his name be remembered no more."

20 O Lord of hosts, righteous judge,
Who tests the reins and the heart,
Let me see your vengeance on them
For to you do I reveal my cause.

Divine Response

21 Therefore thus God said concerning the people of
Anathoth who seek your life and say "You shall not
prophesy in God's name lest you die by our hand":

22 . . .[7] I will punish them. The young men shall die
by the sword. Their sons and daughters shall die
from famine.

23 And there shall be of them no remnant, for I will
bring disaster upon the people of Anathoth, in the
day of their visitation.

FOURTH PRAYER: 20:7-11

The Prayer

7 You have enticed me, O Lord, and I was enticed;
You have used force and prevailed.

---

name is probably to be so construed here also; but if so, the following
verb must be read as a second person: *hoda'tani.* "You informed me" is
likewise required by the parallel "You made me aware."

[6] Reading *beleḥo,* with the omission of one letter.

[7] The clause here omitted is in place where it occurs in the preceding
verse.

Meditation

Daily I have been an object of ridicule;
Everyone taunts me.

8 As often as I speak I must cry out,
Must announce violence and destruction.
The word of the Lord has become for me
A constant source of shame and disgrace.

9 If I say, "I will not remember him
Or speak any more in his name,"
It is in me as a raging fire;
It is pent in my bones;
I weary myself to contain it—
But in vain.

10 I have heard the calumny of the multitude,
Terror on all sides:
"Inform! Let us inform on him!"
Even my [presumed] friends
Watch for me to slip:
"Perchance he may be enticed and we can overpower
him
And take revenge on him."

The Discovered Response

11 But God is with me, this tyrannical power;
Therefore, my persecutors will stumble and fail,
Will suffer great shame in their failure,
An unforgettable, eternal disgrace.

FIFTH PRAYER: 15:10-11,[8] 15-20

Preface

10 Woe to me, my mother, that you bore me,
A man of strife and contention on all sides!

---

[8] Verses 12-14, which have much in common with 17:1, 3, and 4, are an intrusion in chapter 15.

I have been neither a lender nor a borrower
Yet everyone curses me.

The Prayer

11   Indeed,[9] O Lord,
     I have served you well;[10]
     I have interceded with you on behalf of the enemy
     In the time of calamity and the time of disaster—
15   You know [of it].
     Lord, remember me and take notice of me,
     And avenge me on my persecutors.
     Being long-suffering, take not my life.
     Know that for your sake I have borne disgrace.
16   When your words presented themselves I devoured
         them,
     And your word was a pleasure to me . . .[11]
     Because I am called by your name,
     O Lord, God of hosts.
17   I sat not in the company of merrymakers
     Exulting in the joy of my heart.
     I sat alone because of your irresistible power,
     For you filled me with gloom.
18   Why must my pain be perpetual
     And my wound incurable, refusing to heal?
     You are to me verily as a deceptive stream,
     As undependable waters.

Divine Response

19   Therefore thus God said:
     If you repent I will take you back—
     You may minister to me.

[9] See Third Additional Note, p. 241. The Hebrew word is to be read
'amen and God is addressed; note the second person pronoun which
follows.
[10] The verb is to be read *sherattika* with vowel changes.
[11] The words "in the joy of my heart" appear in the Hebrew text at
this point; in the translation here proposed, in the following verse (so
Volz, *Kommentar z.A.T., Jeremia* [Leipzig, 1928]).

You may be my spokesman
Only if you distinguish the worthy from the base.
Let them be drawn to you—not you to them.

20 Then I will make you against this people
As a fortified wall of bronze;
Though they contend with you they will not prevail,
For I will be with you to save and deliver you,
God said.

SIXTH PRAYER: 12:1-2, 4b,[12] 3, 5

The Prayer

1 You have to be in the right, O Lord, if I argue with you!
Nevertheless I will bring certain cases to your attention.
Why does the way of guilty men prosper?
Why are all they secure that deal treacherously?

2 You have planted them and they have taken root;
They go on producing fruit—
They who speak glibly of you
Though you are far from their reins—

4b For they say: "He sees not our ways." [13]

3 [But] you know me, O Lord; you see me;
You try my heart [which is at one] with you.
Deliver them as sheep for slaughter;
Ready them for the day of slaughter.

Divine Response

5 Running with men you get all worn out;
Would you then race with horses?
And if even in a land at peace you fall down [14]
How would you do in the jungle of the Jordan?

[12] Only the concluding words of 12:4 appear to be an original part of this prayer; the remainder of the verse has reference to the distress of a land suffering from drought and may be related to 14:1-6.

[13] The reading "our ways" for Hebrew "our latter end" involves the rearrangement of two letters.

[14] See G. R. Driver in *Studies in Old Testament Prophecy Presented to T. H. Robinson* (Edinburgh, 1950), p. 59.

It is not a surface thing readily apparent, yet a drama
of a human soul unfolds in these six passages and though
the analysis is intricate it rewards the effort.

The heart of each of these passages is the prayer (which
once gives way to meditation). In the prayers four elements can be distinguished: (1) the address, (2) the
expression of confidence, (3) the narrative, and (4) the
plea. The third and fourth of these elements can be divided further: the narrative (3) is either (a) the prophet's
defense of his own conduct or (b) his disparagement of
his adversaries; the plea (4) may be (a) direct or (b)
indirect. The indirect plea is phrased either as a rhetorical
question or as an accusation; in either form it airs a grievance which clamors for redress.

(1) The form of address is invariable. It is always the
proper name of God, in its Hebrew form *YHWH*. It is the
simple vocative: "O Lord," not embellished with attributes. According to the order of the Hebrew words it normally stands as the second word in the prayer—always, at
any rate, among the first three words. The address may,
of course, be repeated later in the prayer. It appears twice
in the second prayer, the second time (in 18:23) again
merely "O Lord"; so, too, in the sixth prayer (12:3). It
appears twice in the third prayer, the second time (in
11:20) in the form "O Lord of hosts." It appears a second
and a third time in the fifth prayer (in 15:15, 16), the
third time again enlarged to "Lord, God of hosts." The
address identifies the passage as a prayer. When a man
addresses words to God we call his words a prayer. The
fourth prayer turns into a meditation in its second half-
verse, after which Jeremiah starts speaking about God,
about "the word of the Lord," and "him" and "his
name." To be sure, a prayer can also have this third

person form; but in such a prayer, as distinct from a meditation, the words are still addressed to God, though indirectly, slantingly: "So may God do! Let God but fulfill the words of your prophecy . . ." (28:6) or "May the Lord bless you and keep you" (Num. 6:24). The six passages in Jeremiah, however, contain no example of the oblique form of prayer—nothing like it except this one meditation. Jeremiah consistently approaches God directly —face to face, as it were—and simply, without adjectives.

(2) To some extent the expression of confidence, the second element in these prayers, makes up for the omitted attributes. Here Jeremiah describes the God whom he addresses—but he does so sparingly. Only occasionally in his prayers this second element appears. "You are the object of my praise," he says in the first prayer, and "You are my refuge in a day of distress" (17:14, 17). In the middle of the third prayer he resumes his address to God: "O Lord of hosts" and adds the words "righteous judge, who tests the reins and the heart" (11:20). In the fifth prayer he addresses God as one who is "long-suffering" (15:15b). And that is all.

Closely viewed, these phrases are no simple listing of divine attributes, no doxological recital. Here, in prayer, Jeremiah considers how matters may stand between him and his judge. This God should know that his prophet both appreciates him ("You are the object of my praise") and depends desperately on him ("You are my refuge in a day of distress"). If it is a question of justice, Jeremiah also has confidence that this "long-suffering," "righteous judge, who tests the reins and the heart," will indeed not fail him. His hands being clean, he speaks to God confidently when he says: "You know what comes from my lips; it is ever before you" (17:16b). He does not fear—he

welcomes a judge before whom one's inmost thoughts and
every deed are bared.

(3) Narrative and plea make up by far the greatest
parts of the six prayers. Such information as litigants at
court seek to read into the record constitutes the narrative
element of the prayers. A litigant both protests his own
exemplary conduct and recites the nefarious doings of
his adversaries. Jeremiah talks in his prayers like such a
litigant.

(a) Protesting his innocence Jeremiah makes himself
out a victim. On this score it is difficult for him to overstate
his case. What he endured in his turbulent life is on record—the indignities, the dangers, the loneliness, and the
suffering. As the reading of the biographical material has
revealed, his adversaries gave Jeremiah wide room for
complaint. But Jeremiah was not aware that he had offended—offended either them or his God.

In the first of these prayers (and in the second and the
fifth) he combines his two denials: "I have neither sought
to escape serving you nor desired the grievous day" (17:
16). He has done what his role as prophet required, and
his God can not reproach him that out of distaste for his
mission he has avoided it. But he has not wished for the
ruin which as God's messenger he has foretold—and
neither can the people reproach him that he has hastened
the "day." "Remember," he says to God again, "how I
have stood before you to speak good on their behalf, to
avert your anger from them" (18:20). Out of love for
his people and with no sense of guilt towards his God, he
has prayed for them. There was more evidence to this
effect. The statement occurs again among these prayers:
". . . I have served you well; I have interceded with you

on behalf of the enemy [Israel] in the time of calamity
and the time of disaster" (15:11).[15] Far from wishing them
ill he had interceded for them. In combination and sepa-
rately he denied offending either men or God. This "gentle
lamb led to the slaughter" (11:19) had not by any kind
of dealings in the market place given men cause for envy
or claim. "I have been neither a lender nor a borrower,"
he says to his mother in the preface to the fifth prayer
(15:10). And in view of his undeserved suffering at the
hands of his persecutors he can ask aggrieved: "Is good
to be rewarded with evil?" (18:20a). So, too, with God,
whom he obeyed even at great cost to himself:

Know that for your sake I have borne disgrace.
When your words presented themselves I devoured them,
And your word was a pleasure to me . . .
Because I am called by your name. . . .
I sat not in the company of merrymakers
Exulting in the joy of my heart.
I sat alone because of your irresistible power,
For you filled me with gloom (15:15-17).

In all respects Jeremiah was blameless.

(b) Not so his opponents. In the narrative element in
his prayers Jeremiah enlarges upon their vicious behavior.
It is not merely that they curse God's prophet, Jeremiah
(15:10), that they taunt him ("Lo, they say to me: 'Where
is this word of God? Let it come to pass'" [17:15]), and
he must endure their ridicule ("The word of the Lord
has become for me a constant source of shame and disgrace" [20:8]). They are just as offensive in their behavior
towards God: They "speak glibly" of him though he is
"far from their reins" and "say: 'He sees not our ways'"

15 See above, p. 85, n. 6.

(12:2b, 4b). God knows that they are two-faced; God
has indeed warned his prophet against them:

> You informed me, O Lord, and I perceived it.
> You made me aware of their doings (11:18), [saying:]
> "Even your brothers, those of your own household,
> Even they have deceived you;
> Even they have loudly declaimed against you.
> Trust them not though they speak of you amiably" (12:6).

They are treacherous as well as hypocritical:

> I have heard the calumny of the multitude,
> Terror on all sides:
> "Inform! Let us inform on him!"
> Even my [presumed] friends
> Watch for me to slip:
> "Perchance he may be enticed and we can overpower him
> And take revenge on him" (20:10).

Their plotting was no innocent sport:

> They said: "Come, let us plot against Jeremiah,
> For teaching has not departed from the priest
> Nor counsel from the sage, nor the word from the prophet.
> Come, let us smite him on the tongue
> And hear no more of his words" (18:18).

They planned violence against him for poaching on their
preserves; they were going to fall upon him and shut his
arrogant mouth. But they were not going to stop with
that; his life was their quarry. They said to him in Anathoth: "You shall not prophesy in God's name lest you
die by our hand" (11:21). They said of him: "Let us
destroy the tree in its sap; let us cut him off from the land

of the living that his name be remembered no more" (11: 19b). Though God knows, Jeremiah yet tells him about it: "They have digged a pit to take me and hid snares for my feet. You know, O Lord, that they plotted my death" (18:22b-23a).

Two questions arise in connection with this narrative element in these prayers of Jeremiah. One concerns their content, the other their form. The one: starting from the circumstantial details here, is it possible to determine at what stage in his life Jeremiah composed these prayers? Attempts have been made to date them as a group and severally but the results have not been convincing. Only this much seems sure, that the experience of the prophet had already assumed its pattern of frustration and suffering. And this could hardly have occurred before the happenings early in the reign of Jehoiakim, the trial for heresy, Jeremiah's years in hiding, the burning of his book (chapters 26, 36). It is hard to say which, if any, of the similar subsequent events had gone into the shaping of this pattern, whether he wrote these prayers still later, in the last years of the kingdom, under Zedekiah, or after the fall of Jerusalem in the time of Gedaliah. The total absence of references to the national scene and the grave political events of those years would suggest that the prayers antedate the siege of Jerusalem in 588. Without trying to be more specific than that, we would assign them to the time between 606 and 588, between the burning of his book and the attack upon Jerusalem. It was in that period that the events occurred which are mentioned at the beginning of Chapter III above—when, for example, Jeremiah was flogged and put in stocks, when he had the altercation with the prophet Hananiah. Jeremiah would have been fifty years old or more.

The second question: Why did Jeremiah tell all of his troubles to God? Not because God was uninformed. It is not Jeremiah who is informing God of these conditions and circumstances; God first revealed to Jeremiah a part, at least, of his knowledge of the treachery of the supposed friends. "You informed me, O Lord, and I perceived it. You made me aware of their doings," he says (11:18). He reports also what God said "concerning the people of Anathoth who seek your life" (11:21). God even warned him about the treachery of his brothers, the men of his own household (12:6). He was an innocent "led to the slaughter, not aware that they were plotting against" him (11:19). God knew of it before he did. Accordingly, when he speaks to God of these things he does not inform God, he reminds him of them: "You know, O Lord, that they plotted my death" (18:23a).

It is the same when Jeremiah speaks of his own conduct. God knows; he has only to be reminded. "You know what comes from my lips; it is ever before you," he says in prayer (17:16b). "You know me, O Lord; you see me; you try my heart [which is at one] with you" (12:3a). "Remember how I have stood before you to speak good on their behalf, to avert your anger from them" (18:20). ". . . O Lord, I have served you well . . . interceded with you on behalf of the enemy . . . —you know [of it]" (15:11, 15). All of this is quite understandable, since the God of Jeremiah is one "who tests the reins and the heart" (11:20). In another context in Jeremiah this same God asks: "Can a man conceal himself in secret places where I will not see him?" (23:24a). It is not necessary to tell one's troubles to a God before whom all is wholly revealed. Obviously a different reason prompted Jeremiah to put all of these matters in array before God. The reason is not remote; according to his serious intent Jeremiah was revealing his cause to his divine judge, hoping for a favorable verdict: "O Lord of hosts, righteous judge, who tests the reins and the heart . . . to you do I reveal my cause" (11:20). He was bringing "certain cases" to God's attention (12:1). It was to him as though in his prayer he was addressing the court; this was the form of his prayer—a presenting of evidence to a judge or jury. And the form carried with it a compulsion, the need to say all of it, regardless of the fact that the judge was in truth the all-knowing God.

Both the form and the language of the prayers evoke the image of the law court. Jeremiah addressed God as a "righteous judge," *shophet zedek* (11:20). He referred to his affair as a "cause," a "case at law": "to you do I reveal my cause" (*riv,* 11:20). He referred to his adversaries not merely as his "persecutors," "them . . . that persecute me" (*rodephai,* 15:15; 17:18) but more pointedly also as his antagonists, "them that contend with me" (*yerivai,* 18:19), here employing a word with unmistakable juridical overtones. And the "guilty men" (*resha'im*) of whom he spoke when he brought "certain cases" (*mishpatim*) to God's attention (12:1) were persons who, according to his view, must receive an adverse verdict—who were in the legal sense "guilty."

Jeremiah, in the imagined role of defendant at court, argued his case before God in prayer, even as he did in the human court before the princes and the people when he had been accused of sedition (26:12-15).[16] The procedure is that described in a deuteronomic law, the procedure followed when a man must defend himself against the accusations of false witnesses (Deut. 19:16-19a). And

[16] See above, pp. 16 ff.

as considerations in Chapter IX will suggest,[17] God's response here is introduced with the term *laken*, "therefore," a word suitable for the transition to a judge's verdict.

The conception that God hears cases and judges them is, of course, by no means foreign to the Bible. It is related to such dominant ideas of biblical Judaism as the covenant between God and Israel, the moral nature of God, God's ethical demands, in particular God's demand for justice among men. The mythology of the New Year's ritual, according to which God is thought to hold court each year and to determine the fate of men, is similar, as is the Judgment Day of biblical eschatology. It is as a corollary of God's moral nature that he is the warder of contracts, that they are often solemnized in his "presence," and that he serves as a lasting "witness" to their terms.[18]

Specific evidence that God was viewed as judge appears in such passages as these: "May the Lord judge between me and you" (Gen. 16:5);[19] "The Lord judge between you and me and the Lord avenge me on you, but let my hand not be against you" (I Sam. 24:13),[20] and especially in the challenging word of God's "servant," confident that the divine judge will give him the favorable verdict:

At hand is he who vindicates me [*mazdiki*].
Who dares oppose me? Let us go to court together.
Who has litigation with me? Let him approach.
Lo, my Lord God helps me;
Who can prove me in the wrong [*yarshi'eni*]? (Isa. 50:8-9a).

[17] See below, p. 133.
[18] See Gen. 31:46-53; I Sam. 12:5; 20:23; Jer. 34:15-19; 42:5; Ezek. 17:13, 19.
[19] Compare Judg. 11:27.
[20] In some editions verse 12; compare verse 16 (or 15) and I Sam. 25:39.

The procedure in the human courts itself reflected the belief in God as judge. Men brought cases to the sanctuary seeking God's judgment. Such is the implication, for example, of the prescription: "Unto the Lord shall come the case of the two of them. And he whom the Lord will sentence shall pay the other double" (Exod. 22:8). Legal decisions reached with the aid of the Urim and Tummim or the ephod were regarded as divine decisions; and sanctuary priests served as judges.

So it was a pervasive thought in Bible times, this thought that God judged a man. And a man could quite naturally appeal to God in prayer even as he would appeal to a human judge for justice. Both the form and the language of Jeremiah's prayers suggest that this prophet directed them to God in his role as judge—not to him as father, or as creator, or as source of natural abundance, or as captain of the hosts of Israel, but in his role as judge. And that is why he told God what was known to him already. Jeremiah's prayer-narratives set out in full array information which God, his judge, being God, knew well without being told, doing so only because in a law court the litigants customarily spread their case before the judge. Jeremiah followed the pattern that belonged in the frame he had chosen for his *tephillah* prayers (if "plea" was indeed the original sense of the word *tephillah* according to its derivation).[21] Jeremiah set forth his case—the facts that must demonstrate his own innocence, his adversaries' guilt—and entered his plea. God must let the facts speak for themselves:

> Give heed to me, O Lord [he demands],
> And hearken to the voice of them that contend with me
>   (18:19).

[21] See Second Additional Note, pp. 236-39.

A valuable by-product of the prayer-narrative is the fact that, having set forth his case in full detail, he himself could look at it and reflect upon it—he could listen to what he had said.

(4) The fourth element in his prayers is his plea, the goal and consequence of his narrative. He asks vindication for himself and the appropriate penalty for his foes—the one or the other or the two in combination.

(a) At times the plea is direct and unambiguous. In such a plea the verbs are uniformly imperatives, jussives, or cohortatives. The direct plea occurs in passages in which Jeremiah solicits God's favor for himself, pleads that God treat him with forbearance and mercy:

> Heal me . . . and I shall be healed;
> Save me, and I shall be saved (17:14).
>
> Be not my ruin (17:17).
>
> Take not my life (15:15).

The direct plea occurs also in passages in which the prophet combines his request for himself with his demand for God's wrath upon his persecutors:

> Let them be ashamed that persecute me, but let
>   me not be ashamed.
> Let them be dismayed, but let me not be dismayed
>   (17:18a).
>
> Remember me and take notice of me,
> And avenge me on my persecutors (15:15a).

It occurs finally in those passages in which, unashamed and uninhibited, he simply calls down upon his opponents the detailed horror of God's vengeance:

Bring on them the day of evil,
And destroy them with a double destruction (17:18b).

Deliver up their children to famine
And give them over to the power of the sword;
And let their women be bereft of children and widowed;
And let their men be slain,
Their young men smitten by the sword in battle.
Let a cry be heard from their houses
When you bring a troop suddenly on them . . .
Forgive not their iniquity
Nor blot out their sin from your sight;
But let them be brought to stumble before you;
Deal with them in the time of your anger (18:21, 22a, 23b).

Let me see your vengeance on them (11:20b).

Deliver them as sheep for slaughter;
Ready them for the day of slaughter (12:3b).

In these last quoted passages it is notable that Jeremiah does not love his enemies. And it may seem strange that one so sensitive and concerned as Jeremiah surely was should have known such hatred—should have voiced such hatred in prayer. And there have been scholars indeed who have wanted to omit these expressions as unworthy additions to the prayers of Jeremiah. It must be admitted that these passages do not rise to the level of others reviewed in a previous chapter—passages illustrative there of the prophet's vast love for his people. It is apparent likewise that they contradict other expressions within the prayers themselves—those in which Jeremiah denies that he "desired the grievous day" (17:16) and claims to have spoken good on behalf of the people to avert from them God's anger (18:20) and to have interceded with him for such purpose in times of calamity (15:11).

Whether or not it is offensive to our taste, however, Jeremiah's demand for the requital of his adversaries is so much a part of the matter in which it is embedded that its removal would constitute major surgery. What Jeremiah asks for his foes can not be disengaged from what he asks for himself; his plea can not be separated from his prayer-narrative; the prayers (as will yet appear) can not be parted from the responses which normally follow, and which, in part, refer to his plea for the ruin of his foes. The links are so strong on all sides that it becomes needful to understand rather than to eliminate this phase of his plea.

These passages suggest that Jeremiah was human. He lacked that form of saintliness which would have required him to forgive his persecutors. With fortitude he endured the torment and he did not let suffering or personal danger deflect him from a course. But he did not pardon the tormentors. It may be significant and a clue to his personality that he could at the same time hate persons and love people. What his prayers reveal of furious resentments and unforgiving anger can not conceal the deeper currents of tenderness in his nature and his involvement with city and nation—with Jerusalem, "the daughter of his people," and with Israel, "God's flock."

(b) The plea element in Jeremiah's prayers is sometimes less direct, a plea by implication only, either in the form of an accusation or in the form of a bold rhetorical question, neither of which God can presumably allow to pass unanswered.

There are four examples of the accusation among these prayers. The first of them is quite long, and only at its beginning is God addressed. Employing a verb the overtones of which are seduction, Jeremiah says to God: "You have enticed me . . . and I was enticed; you have used force and prevailed" (20:7a). Then, reflecting on the consequences of that initial surrender, Jeremiah speaks as one aggrieved, as one of whose good nature God has taken shameful advantage:

> Daily I have been an object of ridicule;
> Everyone taunts me.
> As often as I speak I must cry out,
> Must announce violence and destruction.
> The word of the Lord has become for me
> A constant source of shame and disgrace.
> If I say, "I will not remember him
> Or speak any more in his name,"
> It is in me as a raging fire;
> It is pent in my bones;
> I weary myself to contain it—
> But in vain (20:7b-9).

The second accusation is similar. It, too, has the form of a narrative; and it is only its challenging content that converts it into an appeal—for release from intolerable conditions. The accusation comes in the second couplet: "You filled me with gloom." Jeremiah is speaking to God:

> I sat not in the company of merrymakers
> Exulting in the joy of my heart.
> I sat alone because of your irresistible power,
> For you filled me with gloom (15:17).

And, again to God, he says:

> You are to me verily as a deceptive stream,
> As undependable waters (15:18b).

Remember that the accusing words are addressed to God by his prophet. The accusations have the form of declarative sentences—the verbs are in the indicative—but they have the sting of commands.

In the last of the accusations Jeremiah seems to be speaking with desperation in his voice. He seems to mean: although I know in advance that one must lose his case who enters into litigation with God, nevertheless I can not refrain from speech.

> You have to be in the right, O Lord, if I argue with you!
> Nevertheless I will bring certain cases to your attention
>   (12:1).

"You have to be in the right" is an accusation and God is the accused. He is accused and judge in one. Just as a human judge must recognize the higher authority of the law which he administers, so God the divine judge does not stand above the principle of justice. When Jeremiah (like Job in a later century) calls upon God to defend himself he is appealing over God to that law which God as judge must administer without partiality. "Shall not the judge of all the earth act justly?" (Gen. 18:25).[22]

Finally, there are three rhetorical questions each of which is the equivalent of an appeal. When Jeremiah asks, "Is good to be rewarded with evil?" (18:20a), his question

---

[22] Jer. 4:10 is a further example of a plea in the form of an accusation. With a change in vowels supported by the Greek, it is the bewildered prophets of the preceding verse who here say accusingly: "Ah, Lord God! You have sadly deceived this people and Jerusalem in saying, 'You shall have peace,' whereas the sword touches the very life." When the foe from the north wreaks havoc in the land, Jeremiah here suggests, the confident prophets, dismayed, will call God to account. Not only has God made fools of them, they will complain, but also he has deceived his people—a situation which calls for redress. Like those in Jeremiah's prayers, this accusation, too, is a plea by indirection.

is to be understood in its context. The "good" which he has in mind is immediately specified; it is his efforts to avert God's wrath from those who have now become his accusers. And the "evil" with which the beneficiaries of his generosity have rewarded his beneficence is also detailed. They now "have digged a pit to take [him] and hid snares for [his] feet" (18:22b). The only answer which his question demands is a rectification of the woefully apparent injustice. "Is good to be rewarded with evil?" is no less a plea than are the direct words which soon follow: "Forgive not their iniquity. . . ."

The second rhetorical question is: "Why must my pain be perpetual and my wound incurable, refusing to heal?" (15:18a). The context of the question proves that the pain and the wound are not of the flesh; the pain and the wound are symbols only of the anguish of Jeremiah's spirit. The source of this anguish appears to be his dilemma —his inability to get away from God. The only answer God can give is to dismiss him from his service. It is for release that he here appeals—not directly, to be sure, but by implication. And the implication is strengthened by what immediately follows—an accusation so bold and offensive that it can not go unanswered. The accusation shows that it is of God that he is thinking when he speaks of his pain. The rhetorical question is intimately linked to the accusation: "You are to me verily as a deceptive stream, as undependable waters" (15:18b). Together they are a repeated demand that God let his prophet go.

The last of the rhetorical questions is one which is commonly misunderstood. When Jeremiah asks his insistent "Why?" he is not posing the eternal query. He is not asking an idle question in a vacuum. When he asks, "Why does the way of guilty men prosper? Why are all they

secure that deal treacherously?" (12:1b), the overtones of
the words are not theology but indignation. The "guilty
men" who "deal treacherously" are not the hypothetical
prospering evildoers; they are culprits well known to the
prophet, of whose treachery against his own person he has
recently become aware, of whose guilt he is convinced,
and whom now he accuses before the bar of divine justice.
God "who tests the reins and the heart," God the source
of the prophet's own knowledge of their treachery, who
warned Jeremiah: "Trust them not though they speak of
you amiably" (12:6b), is surely not deceived when they
flatter him. Surely God does not need to be told: "They
. . . speak glibly of you though you are far from their
reins" (12:2b). Yet God, for Jeremiah, is a righteous judge
bound to do justice. So when in his indignation Jeremiah
cries out, "Why does the way of guilty men prosper?"
in reality he affirms that justice has miscarried, that God
has proved untrue to his own nature. The question is challenge, accusation, and demand in one. The only acceptable
answer would be action, not words. Jeremiah already
knows that God is just. It is to God's justice that he appeals. This question, too, though a question, is quite as
much of a plea as are the bitter imperatives which follow:
"Deliver them as sheep for slaughter; ready them for the
day of slaughter."

These are the audible elements in the prayers of Jeremiah, the ones which we can examine and dissect. But
there is another. It is not audible, but it is the most important—the most fruitful.

IX

How Jeremiah Listened

At the end of his praying with words Jeremiah listened, and his listening was a very fruitful part of his prayers. His listening made him ready for what followed—for what he took to be God's answers to his prayers.

In quite a different context Jeremiah's biographer recorded an example of the prophet's listening for a word from God. It was after the murder of Gedaliah when Jews had assembled as a company and prepared to seek refuge in Egypt from the expected consequences of that deed. Before they went on they consulted Jeremiah: Was their proposed course pleasing to God, or was it not? According to the biographer's record, the prophet had no ready answer; ten days passed before he replied. "At the end of ten days the word of God came to Jeremiah and he called Johanan . . . and he said . . . 'So said the Lord, the God of Israel, to whom you sent me to lay before him your supplication . . .'" (42:7-9). The implications are clear; Jeremiah really did pray for his people on that occasion. He prayed and then he waited, listening for God's response. We do not know what went on in the mind of the prophet during those wakeful hours of listening, what wrestlings, what wish-thoughts and what misgivings. All

we have is the result; in God's name, with no uncertainty
and no ambiguity, Jeremiah delivers God's reply to the
questioners: "So said the Lord. . . ." His listening had
yielded fruit.

Jeremiah's listening when he prayed for himself was
also productive. Consider again the six prayers; regard
them now each in its entirety and one after the other.
All are composed of the elements distinguished in the
foregoing chapter, but each contains these elements dif-
ferently arranged and with no pattern apparent. Some
contain these elements and nothing more; some add the
wordless element, the silence which is the prophet's listening, together with its consequence, the divine response,
the answer to his prayer. The passages have been in-
spected in bulk; it remains to see whether they can be
ordered in a procession.

The initial survey afforded a view of the single elements
which make up these prayers:

The address,

The expression of confidence,

The narrative: Jeremiah's defense of himself and
indictment of his adversaries,

The plea: his undisguised demand that his judge vindicate him and damn his enemies, and the same appeal
more subtly phrased as accusation or as loaded question.

The address is a turning to God; it is like "my Father" in
the mouth of the people—itself a declaration expressive of
loyalty. It is like the people's word: "Here we are; we
have come to you" (3:22).[1] When to the address Jeremiah

[1] See above, pp. 102, 104.

adds the expression of confidence, the second element, he puts himself in the position of client and asks God, as it were, to behave in a properly responsible manner to him submissive and dependent. Add the third element and the fourth and it is clear that the prophet is presenting a case. An aggrieved man comes before his judge, seeking "justice." Jeremiah says that he, well-intentioned and without reproach, has fallen victim to unscrupulous men and is in mortal danger; and he says that God should deal with these offenders in his anger and thus save and vindicate his prophet.

Now this analysis and this statement of the content and nature of Jeremiah's prayers are right as far as they go, but they are also an oversimplification. Jeremiah's was a more complicated personality than this statement suggests, and what Jeremiah says he wants may or may not be what in fact he wants. According to this oversimplified statement Jeremiah brings to God's attention those men who cause him grief, and thinks so to be relieved of his distress. What the statement leaves unnoticed is the fact that men are only incidentally the source of his troubles; actually his grievance is aimed more properly at his God—and that is an embarrassing fact because there is no ready cure for such a complaint. Yet this fact indeed emerges when one carefully reads the prayers in a certain order and when one pauses to reflect and to listen even as, seemingly, Jeremiah paused and listened at the end of his prayers, and when also one looks at the divine answers, which are baffling unless reflection has prepared one to read them as answers.

Look again at the six passages in the suggested order; they are translated and arranged for the purpose on pages 106 to 111 above. Watch now for the growing stress Jere-

miah gives to the thought that God is to blame for his
prophet's pain. Watch, finally, for what the prophet learns
when he finds that God has served him as an excuse. The
responses to his prayers are the dramatic evidence of new
knowledge, which comes while he listens.

The prayer in chapter 17 ends with no recorded answer.
This first prayer is made up largely of narrative and plea
but it reaches no conclusion in terms of divine response.
Addressing God, the prophet tells him of what people say.
People taunt and mock Jeremiah, because the word which
he speaks for God appears to be an empty word. It is as
purveyor of God's word that he is suffering; God has
brought this on him. Jeremiah has not evaded his duty
to God; yet neither has he wished the evil to come upon
the people that they should so abuse him. He pleads then
for God's help: "Heal me! . . . Save me . . . Be not my
ruin." And he calls for the destruction of his persecutors:
Let them suffer shame and not me; break them, not me.
And that is all, except for the faint breath of confidence
in the three phrases with which he essays, by praise and
the affirmation of his faith in God's justice, to approach
his God and judge: "For you are the object of my praise,"
"You are my refuge in a day of distress," "You know what
comes from my lips, it is ever before you." This prayer in
chapter 17 remains an unresolved cry for help.

To the second prayer also (in chap. 18) there is no recorded response. Jeremiah here merely addresses to God
his grievances and asks for redress. The narrative starts
in a verse prefaced to the prayer and is resumed in the
prayer itself. It reviews the machinations of those who
would silence the prophet, devising devices, setting traps,
even plotting to take his life. Jeremiah speaks briefly here
also of his own inoffensive conduct; he has indeed inter-

ceded on behalf of such as now seek his undoing. The rest is a plea. Introducing his plea powerfully with the bitter question: "Is good to be rewarded with evil?" he calls for God's unrelenting judgment on his adversaries. In this prayer, in chapter 18 too, he gets no further. His plea falls, as it were, on deaf ears.

But the next prayer, the one in the eleventh chapter, comes to a simple and gratifying conclusion—one which turns out indeed to be too simple. The prayer is largely narrative, contrasting the treacherous scheming of the prophet's family and townsmen with his own unsuspecting simplicity. The plea is briefly phrased: "Let me see your vengeance on them." By way of approach to his "righteous judge" he attributes to him justice and complete knowledge of reins and heart, and he himself expresses resignation. This prayer is followed by an answer. It is introduced with a "therefore" (*laken*), in all probability from the language of the law court, the word a judge would use who, having summarized the argument, prepares to deliver his verdict or to pronounce sentence.[2] "Therefore, thus God said concerning the people of Anathoth." God pronounces against them. Like false witnesses [3] the men of Anathoth shall meet the fate that they planned for Jeremiah. God would punish them, destroy them with sword and famine and leave no remnant. Jeremiah might be completely reassured; and he had reason to be quite satisfied with what his prayers had accomplished. His whole wish granted, for some reason still he prayed.

The answer to the fourth prayer is similar but with a variation. This prayer in chapter 20 is more meditation

[2] Such passages as Num. 20:12; II Kings 1:16; 22:19 f. sharpen this impression.
[3] See Deut. 19:18 f.

than prayer. Jeremiah addresses God in only the first half-verse—the rest is reflection. The prayer is a plea, implicit only, in the form of an accusation. The meditation is largely narrative. It concerns his mocking adversaries who would betray him. He is the constant target of their ridicule and scorn. Only public disgrace rewards his labor as God's mouthpiece. The multitude, presumed friend and foe alike, spreads an evil report of him, seeking his ruin, watching for him to make the slip that would put him in their power and afford them revenge—as though he had done aught to merit hostility. The fault, he now suggests, lies not in him but in God. He has said it less clearly in the first prayer; here he comes out with it. It is because he is the bearer of God's word that he must cry aloud, heralding violence and ruin, and it is this word of God that brings him disgrace. So he turns upon God once in thought, in the third person, and once in prayer straightforwardly. "If I say 'I will not remember him or speak any more in his name,' then it is in me as a raging fire; it is pent in my bones; I weary myself to contain it—but in vain." His prayer implements this meditation. It takes the form of a blatant accusation which only an indifferent God could ignore: "You have enticed me, O Lord, and I was enticed; you have used force and prevailed." I am yours, he says to his God, only by virtue of your superior power; you have impressed me into your service. Indirectly, implicitly, this accusation is his plea. There is no plea in this prayer if it is not in these words: "You have enticed me . . . used force and prevailed." But this is indeed a plea and it means: Release me from this burdensome servitude.

Yet strangely enough the response which here he finds as answer to his plea does not provide the escape which he seeks. It does not save him from God; it only arrests his flight. He reaches the realization that, paradoxically, his weakness is his strength. Just because God is "with" him (this tyrannical power which is God) not he but his tormentors shall fail and suffer everlasting disgrace.

There are now two goals to his desire, and the discovered response to his prayer here takes cognizance of both. He learns that he will achieve the one but not without abandoning the other. First of all he longs for victory over his enemies; this with God's help is a realizable goal. So he tells himself: "My persecutors will stumble and fail, will suffer great shame in their failure, an unforgettable, eternal disgrace." This discovered response to his one wish in this prayer-meditation is quite the same as God's answer to his plea in the third prayer: "I will punish them . . . no remnant . . . bring disaster upon the people of Anathoth. . . ." Their positive content is practically the same; it is a satisfying answer to his one demand.

Observe, before looking at the other wish, that though thus far the answer to the two prayers is the same, the "source" of the response to the third prayer differs from the "source" of the response to the fourth. The former begins with the words: "Therefore, thus God said"; it is introduced as words emanating from God himself. The latter has no such introduction; it is a direct continuation of the meditation which has been the chief component of Jeremiah's fourth prayer. The third prayer ends in dialogue whereas the fourth remains soliloquy, and yet the divine answer in the one and the conclusion which Jeremiah reached in the other are the same. It may seem, then, that it was in meditation, as he listened, that Jeremiah heard the voice of God. He listened: he surely did not speak his meditation here in one breath, as it were; be-

fore the discovered response—before the "but" and the
"therefore" of the last verse—surely he paused to listen and
to reflect and it was then that the new note sounded, one
that he had not heard in God's reply to his third prayer.
It had to do with his other wish.

His other wish became explicit in this fourth prayer.
God had forcibly possessed him; now he wanted peace,
wanted God to leave him alone. It was his wish to be rid
of this compulsion, to have no more the need to speak
for God. This is in fact the burden of the fourth prayer.
And the discovered response to this second goal of his
prayers is the new note here. It is to be heard in the opening words of the response: "But God is with me, this tyrannical power; therefore. . . ." This is a different sort of
answer. It is not a granted wish but a second thought.
Jeremiah reins in before the goal and, as it were, withdraws his petition. In this answer which is not an answer
there is the echo of his consecration vision. It is as though
he had just called to mind God's closing words to him
there: "If they fight with you they will not succeed, for
I am with you to save you" (1:19).[4] It is as though recall-
ing he drew back. Burdensome though God's company had
been, to be without God would be worse. It is only with
God[5] that he might triumph over his foes. He could not
have both at once, victory over his enemies and release
from God's service—so he clung to God. What was new,
specifically stated, was his recognition that though he
resented God's hold on him he was not ready for God to
let go. On a different level—in a higher octave—the new

_____
[4] See above, p. 74.
[5] The author of Ps. 73 regarded "nearness of God" as the supreme
value: "Having thee, I want nothing on earth" (v. 25). See Blank, "The
Nearness of God and Psalm Seventy-three" in *To Do and to Teach*
(Lexington: The College of the Bible, 1953).

note was his indecision, his discovery that his declared desire and his ultimate desire were not the same. That was what he found by listening.

The fifth and sixth prayers support these conclusions and carry the thought a step further. Jeremiah grows more keenly aware of his need for God; he comes to value the attachment yet higher.

In the narrative of the fifth prayer (in chap. 15), Jeremiah devotes little attention to his adversaries, saying about them only, "everyone curses me." For the most part he pleads his own merit. He has not deserved the curses of his people; he has had no business dealings with them. Moreover, true to his responsibility, he has even intervened with God on their behalf. So much for them. But God, too, has wronged him. God has betrayed him, and he must complain of God to God. God should know that serving him has brought disgrace upon his prophet. Jeremiah has kept faith. Willingly, gladly, he has served as God's mouthpiece; he has denied himself life's amenities and sat alone filled, by an irresistible God, with grim conceits. Here his direct appeal—"Remember me and take notice of me, and avenge me on my persecutors . . . Take not my life"—is sharpened by his rhetorical question, "Why must my pain be perpetual . . . refusing to heal?" and barbed with an accusation, "You are to me verily as a deceptive stream, as undependable waters!" To this triple plea (direct appeal, grim question, and challenging accusation), God responds with a startling answer—one which appears at first sight to be anything but an answer. Yet the relevance of God's reply becomes keenly manifest once reflection has supplied the unspoken transition from prayer to response. It is marked unmistakably as a reply: "Therefore thus God said." Again the word "therefore"

(*laken*) ties the response to the prayer as a verdict is tied
to a legal argument, and "thus God said" again identifies
the speaker. What follows, then, is God's response, but it
is no divine apology. God does not even properly sym-
pathize with his agonized prophet; the response is a reprimand. The indignant prophet must walk humbly.

Though spoken in God's name, the reprimand which
follows upon this fifth prayer was, of course, mediated by
Jeremiah. He heard it and he recorded it. And our question is: What prepared him to hear this response? He did
not hear it without listening. What was the content of his
listening? Perhaps he thought over the words he had
spoken. To what, now, had he given expression in his
prayer? And to what position had the importunate out-
pouring of his grief brought him at the last? He had given
unrestrained expression to self-pity, and he had been led
to the, for him, untenable position of one who accuses
God of treachery. When pushed to its furthest, his own
reasoning had led him to a conclusion which he could not
accept. In the very process of marshaling his arguments,
stating his case, and phrasing his desires, he has come to a
double realization: that his wishes were not as he thought
—vengeance and vindication are not everything—and that
his arguments have convicted only that party whom he
held to be the aggrieved—none other than himself. This,
if he thought about it, had been the trend of his prayer,
and if he thought about it, the reflection prepared him for
the answer which now he found—a response both relevant
and adequate, though it grants no expressed wish nor contains comfort, but only rebuke:

> Therefore thus God said:
> If you repent I will take you back—

You may minister to me.
You may be my spokesman
Only if you distinguish the worthy from the base.
Let them be drawn to you—not you to them.
Then will I make you against this people
As a fortified wall of bronze;
Though they contend with you they will not prevail,
For I will be with you to save and deliver you . . .

"If you repent"—it is Jeremiah, then, who has strayed. He felt sorry for himself and he had run away. If now God is to be "with" him—and he wants nothing more—then it is he who must come back.

The last of the prayers (in chap. 12) leads to the same end. The narrative here is brief. It speaks of the prophet's hypocritical adversaries, men on familiar terms with a God who in fact is far from their hearts, despite which, planted by God, they are firmly rooted and prosper, and it speaks of the prophet himself: God knows how faithful his heart is. The rest again is a triple plea—a direct appeal: "Deliver them as sheep for slaughter"; a challenging question: "Why does the way of guilty men prosper? Why are all they secure that deal treacherously?"; and a veiled accusation in which he says: You have to be in the right, Lord, if I argue with you! Nevertheless I will call your attention to certain cases. It almost means: You do not play fair.

In this prayer, as in the fifth, the verdict or response of God is at first sight irrelevant, and only when reflection has made the transition does the relationship appear. The accusation and the question conspire to imply that God is quite unconcerned over the sad fate of his prophet and the undeserved success of the prophet's treacherous foes, and that God holds himself above reproach, being right

only by virtue of his unimpeachable authority. But these
implications, too, are inconceivable; hence the reasoning
must be false. The prophet has placed the blame where
he knows that it does not belong. This is the nature of the
reflection which seemingly intervened to prepare Jeremiah
for the discovered response.

The response is not now introduced as such. It comes
suddenly without a "therefore" or a "thus God said," but
only God can be speaking and only Jeremiah can be addressed. Two questions make up the response, questions
which God directs to his complaining prophet, rhetorical
questions like those which Jeremiah has been aiming at
God. The questions contain figures of speech; analogies
are drawn. It is neither possible nor necessary to interpret
the figures in detail, for, like most biblical metaphors,
these are only partially applicable. The biblical poet observes a common element in the object and its analogue,
and that suffices, and he creates a symbol. Two questions
in symbolic language phrase God's verdict. The verdict
is an admonition: it directs the prophet's gaze back to
himself. Jeremiah must look within to discover the cause
of his misery. The verdict pays no heed to his outraged
sense of justice; it ignores those treacherous ones whose
death the prophet has demanded—ignores as well his implication that God has let him down. It says that not God
but he has failed. It looks at Jeremiah and it sees him as a
man too small for his task, needing to escape, loading on
others his own inadequacies. The words are high poetry;
the meaning resides in the total impression.

> Running with men you get all worn out;
> Would you then race with horses?
> And if even in a land at peace you fall down
> How would you do in the jungle of the Jordan?

Some progress in thought appears within these six compositions. Consider them as three pairs in the sequence followed above. In the first pair, the compositions in chapters 17 and 18, Jeremiah finds no answer to his prayers beyond the faint breath of general confidence which he himself brings to them: "You are my refuge in a day of distress" (17:17). The second pair, those in chapters 11 and 20, conclude with a kind of an answer, one of the two concluding with words attributed to God; the other, with phrases extending the prophet's own meditation, but both having the same import despite this formal difference. Both give Jeremiah the favorable verdict; each is a sentence of doom on his persecutors. But the meditation adds a new factor: Jeremiah complains of abuse at God's hands, yet would choose to have God with him. The answer which he found in the first of this pair—the sentence of death on such as sought to compass his death—was comforting indeed but it was too simple to satisfy his probing spirit. And the meditation, the second in this pair, brings him to realize that his struggle is not with men alone; the true source of his troubles is the power which God has over him. Nevertheless, he is unable to extricate himself from God's hold on him, and he makes the best of it. It is the fact that God is "with" him, he concludes, which gives him the assurance that his adversaries will fail.

The conclusion at this point, his recognition of the value which he attaches to his having God, is the transition to the third and last pair, the compositions in chapters 15 and 12. These two, complete with time for listening and with God's response, with an intricate self-analysis intervening between prayer and response, somewhat less concerned than the others with the fate of the prophet's adversaries, further develop the struggle between prophet

and God, more daringly and penetratingly place the final
blame not on human foes but on God, and end as they
must with the insight, born in anguish of spirit, that the
prophet, not God, is imperfect, that the ultimate source
of the prophet's misery is his own weak will.

Jeremiah addressed his prayers to a God who hears, a
God before whom a man may state his case confident that
justice will be done. He set forth in plain words the matters
that troubled him, listing his grievances, evaluating his
conduct, giving uninhibited verbal expression to his desires. Then he stopped to listen, and the silence was
fraught with heavy consequences. For out of the silence
there came to him fortitude and a purification of his
desires.

When Jeremiah was done with praying, when, too, he
had vented his unreasoned rage against the day of his
birth and the bearer of the tidings of his birth and had
aired a yearning for extinction—his mother his grave—
when after that he thought of it, this Jeremiah was clear-
eyed enough to see himself as one too tender for a prophet's role and to view his words as a man's solicitude for
his own person—as a hymn of self-pity.

But if Jeremiah felt sorry for himself he was not alone
in this. God knew regret as well as he.

X

The Theme of Self-Pity

Two more prophetic figures are among the biblical personages that give expression to self-pity. One of these is Jonah and the other Baruch, Jeremiah's friend; and self-pity is also otherwise associated with the writings of Jeremiah—which facts together justify a closer look here at this theme. Actually the closer look reveals the somewhat startling fact that even the idea of divine self-pity falls within the conceptual range of biblical man.

In the concluding verses of the book of Jonah God says in effect to his reluctant prophet there:

> You are terribly upset about that plant, which cost you no pains at all, which you did not cultivate, which grew overnight, and faded overnight; but what of me? Should I not be distressed concerning this teeming great city, Nineveh . . . ? (Jonah 4:10 f.)

N.B.

It is superficially clear that God, with these words, rebukes Jonah for his desperate anger. Jonah, he suggests, is concerned only for his personal comfort and is now experiencing an attack of self-pity—and merely because a plant, the source of his comfort, has failed him. This much is openly

143

stated; the rest is implicit, lurking in the form of the sentence.

In form, the words of God to Jonah are an argument *a minori ad majus*,[1] the *ḳal waḥomer* of rabbinic literature, and, as is often true when this type of argument occurs, the argument here is elliptical. Before the implications become entirely clear, we have to supply the missing terms (in italics below). Fully stated, the argument would read: "You are terribly upset about that plant, which cost you no pains at all,[2] which you did not cultivate, which grew overnight, and faded overnight, and should I not be distressed concerning this teeming great city, Nineveh, *which cost me no end of toil and which I did care for— for many long years?*" When we have supplied the missing term in this argument in this manner, universalism (God made and cares for Nineveh!) mingles with anthropomorphism (It was no easy task!). But perhaps the least expected new facet of the argument, when thus fully stated, is the implied similarity in *mood* between God and Jonah. Jonah here is not the only one subject to disappointment and distress. Naught but the quite unlooked-for repentance of king and people had saved Nineveh and thus had spared God the personal hurt, the regret that goes with frustration, with unavailing toil and care unrewarded.

But this occurrence of the thought that God is subject to the distress of frustration, here in this verse at the end of Jonah, is not unique. It is also the whole point of that little gem of a chapter in Jeremiah, the forty-fifth, in which Jeremiah comforts his fugitive friend, the companion of his years in hiding, the scribe Baruch. This chapter is a

[1] See T. H. Robinson, *Handbuch z.A.T., Die Zwölf kleinen Propheten* (Tübingen, 1938), p. 126.

[2] For this meaning of the root *'amal*, compare, for example, Jer. 20:18 and Ps. 127:1.

perfect parallel to the end of the book of Jonah. God's word to Baruch is no less a rebuke than his word to Jonah, and the logic is quite the same—only clearer, because here wholly explicit. Paraphrasing in part, we may so restate God's word to the prophet's disciple: "You, Baruch, are saying 'Alas! and Woe! God has added misery to my pain; I am worn out with my sighing and find no respite.' Well, now, consider! What I, myself, built I am about to demolish. What I planted I am about to uproot . . . and would you seek personal advancement? Desist." At the end, with a promise God softens the rebuke: "I will bring disaster down upon all flesh, God says, but I will give you your life as reward wherever you go." [3] But it is the rebuke which carries the theme of self-pity. Pared of unessentials, God's ironic question to the complaining disciple is merely this: "What is your hurt, O man, compared to mine?" And here, too, the thought: It is not men only who experience the personal hurt that stems from frustration. [4] Thus, in a way, the Baruch chapter is the key to the meaning of God's rebuke to Jonah.

And the prayers of Jeremiah are the key to the Baruch chapter. It was Jeremiah's converse with God which taught him what to say to Baruch. Baruch's lament echoes Jeremiah's prayers. Encountered after a review of Jeremiah's prayers, Baruch's "Alas! and Woe!," his holding God accountable ("God has added misery to my pain"), his airing of his grief ("I am worn out with my sighing and find no respite") have a familiar ring. Our understanding of Jeremiah's own experience in prayer has prepared us to understand his disciple's weakness. The source of

[3] Jer. 45:3-5, see above, p. 32.
[4] Here I find myself in agreement with M. Buber, *The Prophetic Faith* (New York: Macmillan, 1949), p. 167.

Jeremiah's answer to Baruch's lament was twofold; it was what he himself had heard when in prayer he had listened, and it was something else. In God's reply to Baruch which Jeremiah mediated, one of the things which God says echoes very clearly God's answers to the prayers of Jeremiah. To himself Jeremiah heard God say: "You may be my spokesman only if you distinguish the worthy from the base" (15:19), and this word forced him to think of relative values and to see things in proportion. And he also heard God's reprimand in the form of a rhetorical question: "Running with men you get all worn out; would you then race with horses?" (12:5), and so he had learned where the fault lay and whose the weakness was. Having himself achieved such insights he was prepared to mediate that part of God's answer to Baruch which appears in the form of a question and a charge. "Would you seek personal advancement?," God asks of Baruch. "Desist," he says.

To be sure, Baruch had not spoken of "personal advancement" in so many words. At the most he had in his lament wished for respite from his sighing—only that. But Jeremiah had learned to listen for the overtones. In the prayers of Jeremiah reflection had supplied the transition from prayer to response and had put the prayer in its proper light, so that God could reply to the unsaid along with the said, could reply to the sense as well as the words and still be understood. So here, too, the reflections of Jeremiah, or of Baruch, or of the two in harmony, translated the "misery," the "pain," the sighs of Baruch, saw them as Baruch's concern for personal comfort and private ambitions, saw them as disproportionate concern when set against an impending common grief, saw them as unworthy in a man with tasks like his; and it was these reflections which prepared the way for the now relevant question, "Would you seek personal advancement?" and for the charge, "Desist."

But there is a part of God's reply to Baruch for which the prayers of Jeremiah afford no parallel. That is the part of his answer in which God expresses regret that he must do what he will do: "What I, myself, built I am about to demolish. What I planted I am about to uproot." These words are, indeed, the expression of divine regret, for they have relevance only against Baruch's lament: "Alas! and Woe! God has added misery to my pain; I am worn out with my sighing and find no respite." As in his reply to Jonah, here also God matches a man's complaint with his own. But this divine regret is not among the features of Jeremiah's prayers. Jeremiah's awareness of God's hurt had a different source.

It was because he himself cared, that Jeremiah knew that God cared also. The parallel to God's regret is not the prayers but the elegiac mood in the lamentations which Jeremiah spoke when he contemplated the ruin of his people. These laments are a striking component of Jeremiah's writings (see Chap. VI, above).

> . . . Grief overwhelms me. I am sick at heart.
> . . . I am utterly broken in the breaking of the
>   daughter of my people;
> I am sunk in gloom, desolation has seized me.
> . . . Would my head were water
> And my eyes a spring of tears!
> I would weep day and night
> For the slain of the daughter of my people (8:18, 21, 23).

This is affliction indeed, and I bear it (10:19b).[5]

[5] See above, pp. 86 f., 90.

Such were the tones of Jeremiah's grief, and they are hardly to be distinguished (this is the notable fact) from those of God's own lamentation—yes, God's—spoken through this same prophet:

I have left my house, abandoned my inheritance,
Given over to her enemies my dearly beloved (12:7).

The similarity is striking, and it is perhaps not strange that Jeremiah, in whom the conflict raged most fiercely, was the prophet who most keenly felt God's hurt.

It goes almost without saying that Jeremiah's God was not aloof. Like Jeremiah, he was most intimately involved with his people's sorrow. As David mourned for Absalom, so in another Jeremianic passage God mourns for Ephraim:

Is Ephraim a favorite son,
My own dear boy,
That as often as I speak of him
I have to remember him again the more? [6]
My compassion is aroused;
I yearn for him (31:20).

Jeremiah fell heir to Hosea's mantle and this was among its hues. For, in the same strain God had spoken of Israel through the prophet Hosea:

How can I give you up, O Ephraim;
Deliver you over, Israel?
. . . My heart turns within me,
I am deeply moved (Hos. 11:8).

[6] Compare the concept of compelling love in Gen. 31:30 and the similar use there of the infinitive absolute.

Jeremiah received the spirit from Hosea and he handed it on to the Second Isaiah. So it is no surprise to hear the same longing in the bold language of the prophet of the Exile, when that prophet expressed God's frenzied impatience at the delay of the salvation of his people:

> For a long time I have held my peace,
> Mute, restraining myself;
> Now I will cry out, like a woman in travail,
> Panting and gasping at once (Isa. 42:14).

All three, Hosea, Jeremiah, and the Second Isaiah, were keenly aware of the hurt of God, but Jeremiah felt and articulated it the most clearly. The combination of his elegies with his prayers completes the theme, provides the divine regret to match the man's self-pity.

So the theme begins to assume a pattern. A man complains, bemoans his bitter lot—as Jonah when the plant fades; as Baruch, who can find no rest; as Jeremiah, torn between God and his people—and each one learns—Jonah, through God's rebuke; Baruch, through Jeremiah's word; and Jeremiah, through his own sharing in God's grief—each learns that God also suffers, and this knowledge, presumably, sets him right.

Three times we have found the pattern complete: a man's complaint seen in the context of God's suffering, both elements present and viewed at once.

To be sure, the single elements also appear alone. Elijah, for example, had his bad moments: "I, even I only, am left, and they seek to take away my life," he said (I Kings 19:10, 14). And he sat beneath a broom tree and invited death, in that he said: "Enough now, Lord! Take away my life; for I am no better than my fathers" (I Kings

19:4). The one half of the pattern is there; Elijah plays his part. But that is all; in the ensuing theophany, God does not match with his own the prophet's complaint. And there are many Elijahs in the Bible, notably among the psalmists. Above all, of course, there is Job. If the titan Job felt pity for himself he had sufficient cause, and a comparison with Jonah and his irritation at the wilting of the gourd seems disproportionate. But what differences there are do not conceal the basic similarities. Many bitterly moan—Elijah, Job, the writers of psalms—moan because of their lot but fail to learn what Jonah learned, and Baruch, and Jeremiah: that their grief is matched by God's.

So, too, the other half of the pattern; it also appears alone. In passages already quoted, Hosea, before Jeremiah, and the Second Isaiah after him, gave voice to God's hurt unprompted by evidence of a man's self-pity. This second element in the pattern appears again alone in the opening words of the flood narrative as related in the earlier source: "And the Lord saw that the wickedness of man was great in the earth . . . and the Lord was sorry that he had made man on the earth, and it grieved him to his heart" (Gen. 6:5 f.). We may at first doubt the relevance of this last passage—wrongly, I think. For, here, too, God's grief stems from frustration, his plans having gone awry. He framed the earth to be populated; he did not intend it for a waste. The Second Isaiah meant something like this when he said of God the creator, who, out of *tohu,* an empty waste, made this world: "Not to be an empty waste did he create it. To be inhabited he formed it" (Isa. 45:18). If so, it was then only with regret and grief and a sense of frustration that God could contemplate destroying with a flood his populated earth. "It grieved him to his heart."

In these latter examples the pattern is partial, the one or the other element appearing alone. It has been found complete in the concluding scene in Jonah, in the word of comfort for Baruch, and in the combination of prayers and elegies in Jeremiah. These form the constellation: Jonah, Baruch, and Jeremiah. By what they say or by what is said to them, each in his way illustrates the theme: a man's troubles, matched and dwarfed by God's own hurt.

There is hardly enough of this to stamp it a dominant feature of biblical religion, yet the pattern occurs frequently enough to be recognized. Against human sorrow, a sort of antidote to a man's self-pity, here and there the reminder appears that all is not too well on high; God, too, knows pain.

Now this thought, that God knows pain, the pain of frustration, deserves a second look. Why cannot the lord of creation, the sole author of human history, merely direct events on earth according to his pleasure and spare himself this pain? What is the ineluctable source of his hurt?

The divine dilemma and the grief are the fruit of the conflict between God's justice and his purpose.

Along with Jeremiah the suffering, righteous Job appealed only to God's characteristic justice.[7] The author of Genesis 18 gave classic expression to this first of the two conflicting elements when, with a rhetorical question, his Abraham sharply defined God's nature: "Must not the Judge of all the earth be just?" (Gen. 18:25). "Is it

[7] See Jer. 11:20; 12:1; 18:19 f. and Job 23:3 f.; 13:18.

possible," Abraham seemed to be asking, "that you should
do such a monstrous thing—to slay the innocent with the
guilty, treating both alike?" [8] He all but admonished God:
"Remember, it is only within these limits that you are
free."

In the context of Abraham's question, not treating the
innocent and guilty alike only meant not destroying the
innocent residents of Sodom along with the guilty; it is
this one aspect of justice that Abraham had in mind. But
justice is two-edged. Not treating the innocent and guilty
alike also means not sparing the guilty. In its positive
form, the principle is fully stated in the related eighteenth
chapter of Ezekiel where the principle "the innocence of
the innocent shall be upon him" is supplemented by the
further assertion "and the guilt of the guilty shall be upon
him" (Ezek. 18:20). Whether they were thinking in terms
of communal retribution or in terms of individual retribution, the writers of the Bible expected God, on the one
hand, to reward merit, but, on the other, as surely, to
punish guilt.

Couple with this latter expectation the fact that, for
the most part in the Bible, it rests with men to choose
the way of innocence or guilt, a thought which a Tal-
mudic authority—the first generation Amora R. Hanina—
expressed in the form: "Everything is in the power of
God except the fear of God" [9]—couple these, and the
limits are more clearly drawn. If God must punish and
men may choose, here is a situation which sets bounds to
God's freedom. Circumstances, man-made situations, may
constrain God to visit punishment.

[8] Paraphrasing verse 23.
[9] *Talmud Babli, Berakot* 33b, quoting Deut. 10:12.

It was the operation of this constraint which led God
to say through Jeremiah in the Baruch chapter: "What I,
myself, built I am about to demolish. What I planted I
am about to uproot." God has no alternative, no choice
more. The same constraint would have caused the destruction of Nineveh had it not been for that city's last-
minute change of heart. Constrained again, God brought
on the waters of the flood, though it grieved his heart to
destroy his new-made earth.

This is the first of the two warring elements: God's
justice, which is so much a part of his nature that it limits
his freedom.

The second element, with which the first comes into
open conflict, giving rise to tension and causing distress,
is God's commitment, or, as it is sometimes conceived,
his purpose. It is, for the most part, his commitment to
his people, his purpose with Israel. But it is also his
broader purpose, his scheme of universal salvation.[10] The
prophet Jeremiah was referring to God's constancy in
relation to Israel when he characterized God as *hasid:*

Come back, Meshuvah Israel, God says,
I do not frown on you;
For I am constant [*hasid*], God says,
I bear no lasting grudge (Jer. 3:12).[11]

Though the pre-Exilic prophets repudiated a one-sided
covenant, the people stubbornly insisted that a promise
is a promise and unquestionably one of the Isaiahs thought
in such terms. This Isaiah used the related word *hesed*

[10] See the discussion of the word *zedek,* "[God's] sure purpose," in
Blank, *Prophetic Faith in Isaiah,* pp. 152-56.
[11] Similarly Jer. 31:20; Isa. 49:15; 54:6; 66:9.

for a new covenant with Israel—a one-sided covenant
which would, in fact, be better termed a divine commitment:

> In a sudden burst of wrath
> Momentarily I hid my face from you,
> But now I comfort you with a firm commitment [ḥesed],
> Says God, your redeemer.
> This is to me as the waters of Noah;
> Even as I swore that no more
> The waters of Noah would deluge the earth,
> So I have sworn not to be angry with you
> Or chastise you [more].
> Yea, the mountains may pass away
> And the hills remove,
> But from you my commitment never—
> Not my covenant of peace (Isa. 54:8-10).

A promise is a promise, they insisted; a commitment
is a commitment. God can no more repudiate a promise
than he can be unjust. He cannot be capricious. Constancy is the very essence of God.[12] It is wholly unlike
him to assault a friend, and his encounters with Jacob
on the river bank and Moses on the road to Egypt [13]
are properly viewed as curious vestiges of an ancient demon-
ism long outgrown. For the most part in the Bible, impulse had given way to principle.

The author of Job devised a story to show what inconstancy might lead to. Once upon a time God acted on an
impulse, he tells us, and went on to regret it. The re-
proachful tone of God's words to Satan reveals his regret.
"You persuaded me to attack him without provocation,"

[12] See Num. 23:19; I Sam. 15:29.
[13] See Gen. 32:25-33; Exod. 4:24-26.

God complains (Job 2:3). And the author evolves the plot of the Job story out of the violence done by this impulsive act to the belief in God's constancy, which belief, of course, his hero-victim can never abandon. Job's God must be constant—he cannot abuse a friend, be the friend a person or a people, the people Israel or mankind.

According to the thinking of biblical man, this, then, is a second limitation of God's freedom. And perhaps it should be noted here that the two limiting factors have what may be called a moral quality in common. The requirement that God remain true to his commitment shares with the requirement that he be just, a moral quality. There is no mechanical necessity involved here like that by which natural effects flow necessarily from natural causes, nor any logical necessity like that which makes inevitable the conclusion of a syllogism—no formal or philosophical necessity. What is involved is a moral necessity—a constraint dictated by moral considerations. The two warring elements have this in common—a moral quality. A moral necessity demands that in a given situation a just God will act in a certain way. And in the same situation, a moral necessity restrains a God committed to a different course from acting in that certain way. The consequences of God's moral nature are at variance with his purpose. And thus the stage is set for conflict, tension, indecision, frustration, and hurt.

One such situation is that to which God alludes in his word to Baruch. What he built and now must demolish, what he planted and must uproot, is the very people of whom he said: "How can I give you up, O Ephraim; deliver you over, Israel?" (Hosea 11:8)

There is something satanic about this dilemma. It is the perfect consummation of Beelzebub's plot against

God's creatures, the fruit of his counsel. In Milton's words, the prince of evil said of men:

> [Perhaps yet we may]
> Seduce them to our party, that their God
> May prove their foe, and with repenting hand
> Abolish his own works. This would surpass
> Common revenge, and interrupt his joy
> In our confusion, and our joy upraise
> In his disturbance . . . (*Paradise Lost* ii, lines 368-73).

Though certainly it is no pervasive biblical theme, this mood of "disturbance" is associated with the person of God in a few memorable passages in the Bible. Here (speaking in human terms) the dynamic of God's distress is the inevitable conflict between opposed elements in the divine nature—inevitable in a God thus entangled in the human situation.

The parallel is striking between prophet and God: God's distress stands alongside Jeremiah's. And the effect is striking: the hint of divine tragedy dwarfs the man's grief, lends to the human situation an ultimate perspective. How can a Jonah or a Baruch complain—or a Jeremiah?

Perhaps it is not strange that the prophet Jeremiah was the one to articulate most clearly the theme of divine self-pity. No doubt it was the stress that the prophet knew in himself, the strain between his love and God's demand, that aroused him to an awareness of God's pain. Jeremiah could understand.

It was the conflict within the prophet which, above all, gave him also his knowledge that he spoke for God.

XI

How Jeremiah Knew

The common denominator in the experience of the prophets was the bitter fact that hardly anybody listened to their words. Whether they set out to arouse the complacent or to comfort the despairing, they harvested futility. Not only the first Isaiah,[1] whose metallic tones struck fear, but even the gentle, rhapsodic Isaiah of the Exile [2] had to complain of a people of unseeing eyes and ears that did not hear. Ezekiel's sarcastic comment betrays his bitterness; God told him, he said: "To them you are only as one who sings [3] ditties with a pleasant voice skillfully; they hear your words, yes, but do nothing whatever" (Ezek. 33:32). The first Isaiah sensed the cause of their deafness: the deaf, he had said, were not able to hear simply because they preferred not to hear. "For it is a defiant people, deceitful sons, sons who are unwilling to hear God's teachings" (Isa. 30:9).[4] Man's ability to shut out the unpleasant—not to see, not to hear—may be a biological necessity, but it is the prophet's Sambatyon.

[1] See Isa. 6:9 f.
[2] See Isa. 43:8; 42:19.
[3] Reading the word as the active participle.
[4] See also Isa. 28:12; 30:15.

He stands thwarted on the hither shore. And none had a
deeper sense of frustration than Jeremiah, whose diagnosis
was the same as Isaiah's: "To whom can I speak and
testify and be heard? Lo, their ear is uncircumcised and
they can not listen. Lo, God's word is to them an object
of scorn, they want none of it" (Jer. 6:10).[5]

Though he knew that what he had to say was both
true and important, Jeremiah could convince no one. The
fact that he was priest as well as prophet carried no
weight. He enjoyed no respect which he had not earned,
no authority beyond what he could win for himself. His
was a kind of nightmarish nakedness: he had no framed
diplomas, no transcripts of academic records, no recourse
to colleagues in a conference. By nothing extrinsic could
he command belief.

But since the fate of his people depended upon his
success with them and, specifically, his ability to make
them see that he brought them an urgent message from
their God, and since there was so little time, his mission
had a grim earnestness and his argument was no col-
legiate debate, no matching of wits for empty honors.
If any one had asked Jeremiah: "Why should I believe
you? How do I know you are speaking the truth? How
indeed do you know?" probably Jeremiah would have
had no ready reply. His book contains no reasoned answers to such questions, no marshaling of arguments, no
legal brief. Yet Jeremiah persistently wrestled with the
problem and his book reflects the ongoing agonizing con-
troversy. It contains the raw materials out of which at
this great distance we now can fashion a kind of an answer which he, the prophet Jeremiah, might have found

---

[5] Verse 15 is similar.

for himself, an answer for him to live with, however well
or ill it would have satisfied his scoffing generation.

From the material which his book contains, material
which has largely been surveyed in preceding chapters,
we can now phrase six reasons on the strength of which
Jeremiah might have said: I know. They are our reasons,
not his, but it is his book which contains the stuff of
which they are made.

(1) The argument which was, and is probably still,
the most convincing to the greatest number is the argument based on fulfilled predictions, the proposition that a
prophet can be accepted as authentic when what he
prophesies is realized. But to Jeremiah the pragmatic test
was hardly the most satisfying of his several criteria.

In those days prophets did, of course, give "signs" to
prove their authenticity. The signs were their credentials.
In a form of the exodus narrative which is probably later
than the Second Isaiah and shows his influence, the true
and highly reputed prophet Moses performs successful
signs before Pharaoh to validate his message.[6] In a law
in Deuteronomy the possibility is envisaged that, as a test
of Israel's constancy, even a heretical prophet may propose a sign and the sign come true (Deut. 13:2 f.). To
convince a king, the legendary Isaiah said that the shadow
on a sundial would move backwards—and it did move
ten degrees backwards (Isa. 38:7 f.).

And it would be false to say that even a Jeremiah was
contemptuous of facts and laid no store at all by successful predictions, though he attached higher value to other
evidence. When, in prison, he has a premonition that a

[6] See Exod. 7:8-13; 7:22; 8:14 f.; 9:11 f.; 9:16.

cousin will come to him and offer him the chance to buy
a certain field and when, the next day, his cousin comes
on that errand, Jeremiah himself sees in the act the will
of God—because it happened as, in advance, he knew it
would happen (Jer. 32:6-8).

On another occasion, when he has an opening he says
approximately: "I told you so." Zedekiah the king has sent
for him, fetched him from prison to learn God's word.
And why? Because, of all the prophets, Jeremiah was the
one who had said the Babylonians would come, and they
have come. Jeremiah does not now resist the temptation
to point out the moral: "Where are your prophets who
prophesied for you: 'The king of Babylon will not come
out against you and this land'?" (37:19).[7] He gloats here,
even as on another occasion he challenges: "Any prophet
who prophesies good, when what he says occurs, only
then it is known that God has truly sent that prophet"
(28:9).[8] By the light that is in him Jeremiah foresees the
disappointment which all smug prophets must experience,
whereas he, predicting war, will triumph. There is little
to distinguish his challenge here in anticipation from
his I-told-you-so in retrospect. So, he is not averse to the
proof of fulfillment; it is only that this proof comes for
him too tragically late. It is grim satisfaction to be proved
right by an occurrence which you frantically sought to
prevent.

This, too, must be said (and it is important), that
though fulfillment may prove that a prophet's prediction
was right, nonfulfillment proves only that the specific was
wrong. Isaiah, for example, knew himself right even
though in 701 the army of Assyria withdrew before re-

[7] See above, p. 45.
[8] See above, p. 40, and compare Jer. 17:15; 44:28; and Ezek. 13:6.

ducing Jerusalem (Isa. 22:1-14).[9] Similarly, Jeremiah was
not shaken by the withdrawal of the Babylonian troops
in 587 to meet the Egyptian threat (Jer. 37:9 f.).[10] The
principle behind the prediction may retain its momentous
validity amid the shift of circumstances, and the prophet
whose predictions have gone awry may still have spoken
truth.

Probably, then, Jeremiah had little enthusiasm for the
argument based on fulfilled predictions, what men might
call "success" seeming to him a prop too frail to buttress
his conviction. Nevertheless, he made use of it, needing
all the support he could muster.

(2) Apparently for Jeremiah his strongest argument
is no argument at all, but a simple affirmation. His only
plea before the court when, charged with the capital
offense of heresy, he fought for his life is a simple affirmation. The argument amounts to an affidavit—just that and
nothing more, a bare statement in court:

> "It was God who sent me to prophesy against this house and
> against this city all of the words which you have heard . . .
> I am in your hands; do to me as is right and pleasing to you.
> Yet you must know that if you kill me you take upon your-
> selves the guilt of spilling innocent blood . . . for, truly
> God sent me to speak to you all of these words" (26:12-15).[11]

That is no careless statement; considering the circumstances, we suspect that the prophet had no stronger argument in his arsenal than his own certain knowledge that
he spoke for God. His statement is impressive for its simplicity: "It was God who sent me . . . truly, God sent
me." What more can a man say?

[9] See above, p. 83.   [11] See above, pp. 16 f.
[10] See above, p. 50.

If chapter 26 is an "affidavit," chapter 1 is the nearest thing to a "diploma."

> God said to me, Do not say: "I am a lad"; for wherever I send you you shall go, and whatever I command you you shall speak. . . . And God put forth his hand and touched my mouth. And God said to me, Lo, I have put my words in your mouth (1:7, 9).[12]

It is not, in fact, a diploma; it is a deposition: it bears no one's seal or signature but Jeremiah's own: "God said to me," "And God said to me." [13]

This passage is one of several descriptions of his experience with God. According to these, Jeremiah's conviction was not the conclusion of a syllogism but the result of a religious experience—his Sinai. He has "stood in [God's] private council" (23:22), has been admitted to intimacy with God, shared and mirrored his moods, divine disappointment, divine indignation:

> My heart breaks, I shudder all over;
> I am as one drunk, overcome with wine,
> Because of the Lord, yea, the words of his holiness (23:9).
>
> I am filled with divine indignation,
> Exhausted with holding it in . . . (6:11).

Not in public utterances alone, but in prayer as well he spoke in this manner.

> God is with me, this tyrannical power (20:11).
>
> I sat alone because of your irresistible power,
> For you filled me with gloom (15:17).[14]

---

[12] See above, p. 73.   [14] See above, pp. 76, 110.
[13] See also Jer. 15:16, 19.

Withal, Jeremiah remained very much Jeremiah. What he described is not a mystical union; he held back too much for that, stood apart, and prayed, and dissented. He was not submerged in God; his experience was a sharing: Jeremiah sharing with God.[15]

The second argument, then, the one which he invoked in his moment of greatest need, is the immediacy of his experience. He was taking no one else's word for it: "God said to me." Recognition of the validity of this criterion, it seems, would have saved the life of a "man of God" who paralyzed a king, split an altar, predicted a distant reform, but injudiciously put greater store by a reported word than by his own unmediated experience of God (I Kings 13:17 f.). Unlike that man of God Jeremiah insisted that he had himself walked with God; therefore truly and faithfully he spoke God's word.

(3) Jeremiah eliminated any possible sources for his message other than God. His voice, he said—and that is the third proposition—was not the *vox populi;* he spoke indeed the unpopular word. He left all clichés to the plagiarizers, to the dealers in used oracles, of whom God said: "They contrive to make my people forget my name with their dreams which they repeat one to another" (23:27) and "Therefore, lo! I am against the prophets . . . who pilfer my words a man from his fellow. Lo, I am against the prophets . . . who appropriate phrases and oracularly boast, '[Behold,] an oracle!'" (23:30 f.).

Jeremiah pointedly dissociated himself from the popular prophets. He had not, as they had done, borrowed words of other prophets, nor did he echo the rumblings of the crowd. Indeed, so much at odds with the common

[15] See Chapter VI, above.

belief was his own word that he passed for a madman
(*meshugga'*, 29:26). He withstood "the test of ridicule"—
yet was discredited. Of this he complained to God, the
very cause of his grief:

> You have enticed me, O Lord, and I was enticed . . .
> Daily I have been an object of ridicule,
> Everyone taunts me . . .
> The word of the Lord has become for me
> A constant source of shame and disgrace (20:7 f.).

On another occasion, in a similar context, gently he re-
proached his God:

> Know that for your sake I have borne disgrace (15:15).

> Lo, they say to me:
> "Where is this word of God?
> Let it come to pass" (17:15).[16]

The implications of the record must be clear: the
source of Jeremiah's word is obviously not the crowd.
His voice is not the *vox populi*. What is it then but the
vox dei?

(4) Or does another presumptive source suggest itself?
Could he be deceived; could it be his own voice that he
mistakes for the voice of God? His repudiation of this
alternative is his fourth argument. For two reasons he
must rule out the possibility that the words he speaks
are his own words, not God's.

(a) They are not his own words because no one would
be such a fool as to invite the disasters which his speaking
entailed. What had it got him, this speaking for God?

---

16 See above, pp. 106, 108 f., 110.

Curses and a flogging, another flogging and exposure in stocks, taunts and accusations, arrest and imprisonment, the plight of a fugitive, of a pariah, a life of loneliness.

To speak of "disinterest" would be to understate the case. To the question *cui bono?* he could reply: Certainly I have no profit from my labors. Quite the contrary; the message I bring is my ruin.

This is the argument which, if Plato may be trusted, Socrates also used a couple of centuries later in his futile attempt to prove that God had sent him:

> That I am given to you by God is proved by this:—that if I had been like other men, I should not have neglected all my own concerns . . . and have been doing yours . . . And had I gained anything, or if my exhortations had been paid, there would have been some sense in that; but now . . . not even the impudence of my accusers dares to say that I have ever exacted or sought pay of anyone; they have no witness of that. And I have a witness of the truth of what I say; my poverty is a sufficient witness. (From Jowett's translation of Plato's *Apology*.)

Like Jeremiah, Socrates asked in whose interest, then, he spoke—certainly not in his own. From his condition, each concluded that it was not he but God who set his dolorous way.

(b) Jeremiah for another reason had to repudiate the implication that his words were his own invention, a delusion. That reason was that he would have said quite different things if he had obeyed his own impulse. His speech was not, indeed, automatic; nevertheless it was beyond his power to refrain from speech. He was possessed by a sense of inevitability.

If I say, "I will not remember him
Or speak any more in his name,"
It is in me as a raging fire;
It is pent in my bones;
I weary myself to contain it—
But in vain (20:9).[17]

I am filled with divine indignation,
Exhausted with holding it in . . . (6:11).

Similar again is Socrates' claim and similar his desperate
inability to evoke belief. This is how he put it:

Someone will say: Yes, Socrates, but can you not hold your
tongue . . . ? Now I have great difficulty in making you
understand my answer to this. For if I tell you that this
would be a disobedience to a divine command, and therefore that I cannot hold my tongue, you will not believe that
I am serious; and if I say again that the greatest good of
man is daily to converse about virtue . . . and that the
life which is unexamined is not worth living—that you are
still less likely to believe. And yet what I say is true, although a thing of which it is hard for me to persuade you.
(From the *Apology*.)

Two men claimed they had to speak: the one lost his
case and drank the hemlock; by some magic, the other
escaped.

Yet Jeremiah's plight was sad: he had to speak, and
when he spoke he said only wrong things, for in very fact
he loved his people. His laments, already quoted,[18] have
become familiar:

[17] See also verses 7, 11.
[18] See above, pp. 86-90.

. . . Grief overwhelms me. I am sick at heart . . .
I am utterly broken in the breaking of the daughter of my
    people;
I am sunk in gloom; desolation has seized me . . .
Would my head were water
And my eyes a spring of tears! (8:18, 21, 23a)

. . . If you will not hearken
I must privately weep . . .
And my eyes drop tears
That God's flock is in captivity (13:17).

. . . Broken with an awful breaking
Is the virgin, the daughter of my people . . . (14:17).

. . . This is affliction indeed, and I bear it (10:19).

It is inconceivable that Jeremiah could wish down judgment on a people whom he loved with such tender affec-
tion. He did quite the contrary. He disregarded what he
believed to be God's will with him—did so consciously,
drawn by the stronger tug of love for his people. In a
sense defying his master, he sometimes prayed for them.[19]
Though God had said that he was not to pray for their
good he yet waited on God "to speak good on their behalf"; though he knew himself forbidden he did intercede
"in a time of calamity." And apparently his activity was
known, since both people and king appealed to him to
serve as intercessor.[20]

It was so then; he served his God, said for God what
as prophet he must say, but not because he wished it.
He told God of his loyal reservations:

[19] See Chapter VII, above.
[20] See above, pp. 86, 93 f.

I have neither sought to escape serving you
Nor desired the grievous day (17:16).

No, he was far from desiring the ruin of the daughter
of his people.

And that was the fourth of his proofs. Even as his
voice was not the voice of the crowd, so it was not the
wish-child of his own heart, being the contrary of his
wish for his people. But he admitted no further alternative; it must be, then, the voice of God.

(5) The fifth and sixth of his reasons may be paired.
Together they differ somewhat from the others, being
based on the content of the message. If the prophet had
debated the matter and presented an argument point by
point (which of course he did not do, the formulation of
the reasons being ours), it might be observed that here
he shifted ground and put the case so: Very well, if you
do not choose to believe me, and refuse to accept even
my life as proof; if you will not let me say: "It is true
because it is God's word," then let me say: "It is God's
word because it is true."

As concerns the content of his message, then, he first
denies that it is heresy and aligns himself with predeces-
sors tried and true. He commends the ancient, tested
ways:

. . . Stand by the ways and observe,
Ask of the ancient paths,
Which way [leads to] good, and follow it,
And find your security . . . (6:16).[21]

Jeremiah agrees: God spoke to the fathers when he
brought them from Egypt—it is only that a false, a formal-
istic tradition has arisen concerning what God then said:

[21] See also the obscure passage Jer. 18:15, quoted below, p. 180.

I did not speak with your fathers or charge them when I took them from Egypt's land concerning offerings and sacrifices; this was my charge to them: "Obey me, and then I will be your God and you my people, and follow in the whole way that I shall yet prescribe, that you may prosper" (7:22 f.).

If God asks now to be heard, that is no new-fashioned fancy.

Rejecting the current slogans, Jeremiah yet espouses no upstart heresy; he represents a tradition. It is the many others who are out of step. In the present situation, it is the prophets of peace who have left the road—those prophets who "have found a cure for the impending ruin of my people all too lightly, in that they say 'Peace, Peace!' though peace is lacking" (8:11).[22] Jeremiah regards himself as one in a succession of prophets from "of old" who "prophesied for many lands and great kingdoms of war, disaster, and disease" (28:8). No newfangled notion, no heresy his; he stands with these prophets squarely facing reality, grim though it be. From what he says, from its normative character, one may know that truly God sent him.

(6) And the last of the reasons, referring also to the content of the word, is similar. What Jeremiah says for God is ethical and rational and thus comports with the nature of God; it is what such a God as Jeremiah knows must naturally say. The words are the words of a just and constant God, whose purpose expressed by his prophet is to turn his people, through knowledge of him, into ways of righteousness. "Of this let him boast who boasts: that he understands and knows me, that I, God, act on earth with constancy, justice and righteousness—

[22] See also Jer. 4:10; 14:15; 23:17, quoted below, pp. 206 f.

that I desire these [qualities], God says" (9:23). Jeremiah
elsewhere equates "knowing" God with doing justice and
righteousness, judging the case of the poor and needy
(22:15 f.).[23]

In *The Prophets of Israel*, Moses Buttenwieser, speaking of Amos and Micah, Isaiah, Jeremiah, referred to "the
great basic truths or principles of which they were cog-
nizant through their moral consciousness, and which,
constituting their revelation from God, formed the centre
and essence of their prophecy." [24] Pointing to such "basic
truths," not of his making, without and above and beyond
himself, but nevertheless the content or substance of his
knowledge of God, Jeremiah could say: By these I know,
by these you may know that "truly God sent me."

In Jerusalem Jeremiah had seen adulterous, lying
prophets strengthening the hands of malefactors (23:14).
But God did not send them, he said. Had they "stood
in God's council" they would have exhorted the people
in words designed not to confirm them in their wickedness
but to "deflect them from their evil way" (23:22). Unlike
them, Jeremiah was a prophet who enjoyed intimacy with
God, and as proof spoke a fitting word—"a faithful messenger" to him who sent him. His words bore the imprint
of their divine author.

Once the prophet even seems to say: He is no parochial,
regional God whom I represent; universalize my words
and they will stand the test. They are the words of a God
transcending people and land, who says:

> Am I a God of near-at-hand . . . and not a God of
> far-away?

[23] See also Jer. 7:5 f.; 22:3 (quoted below, p. 187) and 5:28 f.
[24] *Op. cit.*, p. 152.

. . . The heavens and the earth—do I not fill them?
   (23:23 f.).

The prima facie evidence of the message itself is the final argument. The words themselves testify to their authenticity and to the prophet's veracity.

For these several reasons Jeremiah knew that the word which he spoke was the word of God.

Section III

What Jeremiah Said

XII

Flowing Well and Broken Cistern

Jeremiah asked his people to be loyal to their God. Jeremiah appears to have prized constancy, faithfulness, devotion, even for its own sake; that is why he said: "Lord, do you not look for faithfulness?" [1] (5:3) and that is why he approved of the Rechabites. Though it was loyalty to God that he especially prized he lauded the Rachabites for their faithfulness as such. Near the end of the reign of Jehoiakim when the Babylonians were approaching Jerusalem and the nomadic Rechabites sought refuge within the city's fortified walls, Jeremiah tested these people, and they stood the test. Jeremiah's narrative reads in part as follows:

> . . . I set before the members of the Rechabite community full bowls of wine and cups and I said to them: "Drink." But they said: "We do not drink wine, because our founder, Jonadab, Rechab's son, gave us this charge: 'You shall not drink wine, you or your children, ever. You shall not build houses and you shall not sow seeds, and you shall not plant

[1] The Hebrew term is *'emunah.* Concerning the concept "faithfulness," see Blank, *Prophetic Faith in Isaiah,* chapter III.

175

vineyards, you shall have none; for you shall dwell in tents
all your days in order that you may live long in the land
of your sojourning.' And we obeyed our founder, Jonadab,
Rechab's son, in all that he commanded us, not ever drinking wine, we, our wives, our sons and our daughters, and
not building houses to dwell in; and we own neither vineyard nor field of seed, and we have dwelt in tents and have
obeyed and done all that our founder Jonadab commanded
us . . ." (35:5-10).

So then Jeremiah said to his people in Jerusalem: "Will
you not take a lesson?" and he used a favorite word,
musar,[2] but here in an uncommon sense—a painless
lesson (v. 13). "The community of Jonadab, Rechab's
son, kept the charge that their founder gave them," God
said, "but this people has not obeyed me" (v. 16), and
he went on to promise the Rechabites survival as their
reward—a promise comparable to the promises he was
to make to Baruch and to Eved-melech.[3]

The Rechabite episode inspires the nearer question:
For what virtue do God and his prophet reward this community? Was it for what specifically they did or refrained
from doing; for not drinking wine, not living in permanent
homes, not engaging in agriculture? Or was it rather for
the quality of character of which their abstinence was
proof?

It is not impossible that Jeremiah admired the Rechabites for their specific way of life. Possibly these austere
conservatives, holding to their nomadic code, untainted
by the offensive rites then associated with agriculture,
uncorrupted also by the city's greed, approximated Jere-

---

[2] See below, pp. 196-99.
[3] See above, pp. 32, 55.

miah's ideal. Probably, indeed, Jeremiah himself had a nostalgia for the wilderness. Like Elijah who ran away to a cave in the desert,[4] Jeremiah longed to escape from the rapacious society of the capital city to the fancied tranquility of a wilderness lodge.[5] And too, like his spiritual kin, Hosea, who spoke of the wilderness period of Israel's life as a matchless time of harmony between people and God,[6] Jeremiah phrased God's longing as a wistful memory:

> . . . I remember for you the constancy of your youthful
>   days,
> The love of your first married years,
> How you followed me in the desert,
> In a land unsown . . .
> What fault did your fathers find in me
> That they left me
> And pursued a vanity
> And became as naught,
> And did not ask: "Where is God
> Who brought us up from Egypt's land,
> Who led us through the desert . . . ?" (2:2, 5 f.)

So too, in a passage strongly reminiscent of Hosea, Jeremiah spoke of the wilderness as the place of reconciliation:

> In the wilderness it has found mercy—
> The people left of the sword . . . (31:2).

The prophetic opposition to the Baalistic house of Ahab in the ninth century, led by Elijah, Elisha, and Jehu, had the blessing of Jonadab, the founder of the Rechabite

[4] I Kings 19:4-9.
[5] Jer. 9:1-7; see above, p. 77.
[6] Hos. 2:16 f.

order.[7] So there are reasons to associate Jeremiah with the Rechabites, by way of a prophetic succession which included Elijah and Hosea, and possibly his approval of the Rechabites was specific.

But, on the other hand, in his chapter on the Rechabites Jeremiah nowhere suggests that his approval depends upon the specific rules that governed the lives of those men. Jeremiah spoke only of their loyalty as such. He commended them for their lasting faithfulness to an ancient commitment. (It was more than two hundred years from Jehu and Jonadab to Jehoiakim.) In drawing the "lesson" Jeremiah said nothing of the virtue of abstinence and tents or of the sin of agriculture; he only contrasted the constancy of the Rechabites who "kept the charge that their founder gave them" with the vacillation of the people of Israel as a whole: "but this people has not obeyed me." Jeremiah appears to have set a high value upon obedience, loyalty, constancy, as such. And of his people he demanded this loyalty to their God.

He knew constancy to be characteristic of God:

Come back, Meshuvah Israel, God says,
I do not frown on you;
For I am constant, God says,
I bear no lasting grudge (3:12).[8]

I love you with a lasting love;
Therefore I extend you [my] devotion (31:3b).

God was constant, and he could look for constancy in men. Jeremiah could ask: "Lord, do you not look for faithfulness?" (5:3).

[7] II Kings 10, see verse 15.
[8] See above, p. 153, and below, p. 218.

But Jeremiah had to deplore the lack of such faithfulness: "Lost is faithfulness, gone from their mouth" (7:28). Israel's disloyalty, inconstancy, unfaithfulness, took the form of apostasy—a folly which Jeremiah repeatedly deplored. For cheap and worthless imitations Israel had forsaken its God—to Israel's lasting hurt.

> How can I forgive you for this?
> Your sons have abandoned me and have done homage
> to imitation gods (5:7a).

> You forsook me, God says; you go backwards (15:6a).

Prophets prophesying by Baal led the people astray, helped them forget God.[9] Like shepherd, like sheep:

> Because the shepherds are brutish
> And have not sought God,
> Therefore they have not succeeded
> And all their flock is scattered (10:21).

> This is your lot, your measured portion from me, God says,
> In that you forgot me and put your faith in falsehood
> (13:25).

And Jeremiah put the same thoughts also in vivid figures. It is a wholly unnatural thing to forsake one's God.

> Does a maiden forget her adornments,
> A bride her ribbons?
> My people have forgotten me
> Days without number (2:32).

> Therefore so God said:
> Inquire among the nations;

[9] Jer. 23:13, 27.

Who has heard of such things?
The virgin Israel
Has done a most horrifying deed . . .
My people have forgotten me.
They do service to a vanity;
. . . [And they have gone from] the everlasting paths
To go on byways,
A road not built up (18:13, 15).

Once Jeremiah employed Isaiah's figure of the wayward
vineyard,[10] and with like intent:

I planted you as a cultured vine,
A wholly true seed,
But how you have degenerated . . .
Become a freakish plant! (2:21)

With unmatched artistry Jeremiah compared the gods
of nations to the failing waters of a broken cistern as
against Israel's God, who is as the living waters of a flowing well:

. . . I will yet reason with you, God says,
And with your children I will reason.
Cross to the shores of Cyprus and observe,
Send messengers to Kedar and consider well;
Observe whether the like of this has happened.
Has a nation traded gods?
And they are not even gods—
Yet my people has traded its glory
For a useless thing.
Be appalled at this, O ye heavens,
And be horrified . . . utterly, God says,
For my people have done two wrongs:
They have abandoned me,

10 Isa. 5:1-7.

A flowing well,
To dig themselves cisterns,
Broken cisterns,
That do not hold water (2:9-13).

Israel's abandoning its God was folly, indeed a tragic error, as events would yet disclose. Jeremiah once acted out Israel's past, present, and future; and the symbols that he used depict the tragic nature of the circumstances as he saw them. To symbolize the initial intimacy between God and people Jeremiah chose a loincloth. He purchased such a cloth and wore it next to his body (13:2), and he heard God's explanation of the act: "As the loincloth clings to the loins of a man, so I made all the house of Israel and all the house of Judah cleave to me, God says, to be my people and for repute and praise and splendor" (13:11a). The choice of this symbol is fresh evidence of the love for Israel which Jeremiah shared with God. So it was in the past, Jeremiah is saying, and his symbol suggests again the constancy of Israel's "youthful days," the love of the "first married years" (2:2). But now the present—in a single clause: "but they did not listen" (13:11b), and more broadly: "this evil people who refuse to listen to my words, who follow the wilful inclination of their heart and have gone after other gods, serving and worshiping them" (13:10a). And so, the future: Israel's unfaithfulness can have but one tragic consequence. Jeremiah goes with the loincloth to a wild place, disposes of it in a hole in a rock and abandons it there. When, after many days, he returns and recovers it he finds it wholly spoiled and useless (13:3-8). And that is to be the fate of Judah; it, too, will rot abandoned (13:9, 10b).

Judah has compounded the folly. Leaving God was foolish, but seeking out Baal, and Molech, and "the queen of heaven," and strange paths, and manufactured gods, was madness. Defilement "on every high hill and under every leafy tree" (2:20) was beastly; pursuit of alien ways was futile frivolity (3:13); the baking of gingerbread men and the spilling of libations for "the queen of heaven" or "the host of heaven" (19:13; 44:18 f.) was silly; serving abominations, saying "to the wooden thing: 'You are my father!' and to the one of stone: 'You gave birth to me!' " (2:27) was nonsensical; shedding the blood of innocents, sacrificing children in the valley by fire to Baal-Molech (19:4 f.; 32:35) was suicidal.[11] All together such conduct was utterly mad. Such faithlessness could only lead to a permanent rift between God and people.

Unless, of course, there were to be amendment. Jeremiah wondered whether in the nature of things reconciliation was possible. He had in mind a certain law about remarriage after divorce, such a law as is formulated in Deut. 24:1-4, and he devised a metaphor. Alluding to some such formula, Jeremiah asked:

> If a man divorce his wife
> And she go from him
> And marry another,
> May he return to her anew? . . .
> You played the whore with many lovers;
> May you now return to me? God says (3:1).[12]

Jeremiah wondered whether reconciliation was possible; but his question was something of a challenge, and it

[11] See also 2:23; 3:6, 9; 7:18; 8:2.
[12] See also verse 20.

does not suggest that Jeremiah believed the way back to be forever barred.

Repeatedly, indeed, through Jeremiah God called his people back. He summoned them: "Come back, Meshu-vah Israel" (3:12), "Come back, you wayward sons" (3:22). He spoke hopefully of their return: "If you come back, O Israel . . . if you come back to me . . ." (4:1). He experienced the disappointment of their refusal: "I thought: 'After she has done all of these things she will come back to me,' but she did not come back" (3:7a), "They refused to come back" (8:5b), and yet again: "They did not turn back from their ways" (15:7), and once, reservedly: ". . . Judah did not come back to me with her whole heart, but only in bad faith, God says" (3:10). True prophets would "deflect them from their evil way" (23:22); and Jeremiah denounced prophets whose activity only "reassured the wrongdoers so that no one turned from his wrong" (23:14). Unlike those prophets, Jeremiah's concern was to effect reconciliation. "Perhaps," he said; "perhaps [*'ulai*] they will listen and turn each from his evil way" (26:3); that was his motivation for the temple sermon which almost cost him his life. That was his reason, too, for writing the scroll which Jehoiakim burned: "Perhaps" they will "turn each from his evil way" (36:3, 7). Jeremiah, in fact, spoke of his life's work as one single appeal: "Return each of you from his wicked way . . . and so abide in the land" (25:5).[13] Jeremiah believed, then, that the way was open. All that was lacking was "knowledge of God."

Expressed positively, the reason Jeremiah so deplored his people's flirtation with "other gods" was this: that he wanted his people to live what he understood to be

[13] See above, pp. 26, 31.

their authentic way of life, to be true to themselves, to pursue their destiny. Negatively stated, devotion to the "other gods," to Baal, Molech, the "queen of heaven," to the "thing of wood" or the "thing of stone," was not his people's way of life; it was "changing" gods, being untrue, abandoning their destiny. Jeremiah was against assimilation. He was for national self-realization. And the way to this self-realization was through "knowledge of God."

What both God and Jeremiah wanted to implant within the heart of Israel was *da'at,* "knowledge" of God. To Jeremiah knowledge of God meant a willingness and a readiness to follow the pattern of conduct which he took to be God's will.

According to Jeremiah justice was a dominant motif in the pattern—justice along with integrity, faithfulness, and constancy. Jeremiah had a great deal to say about the knowledge of God.

He described the chaos of a society lacking such knowledge. Near the beginning of the following passage, God says: "They do not know me," and at the end he repeats: "They have refused to know me," and that is the basic fault, whatever else is wrong.

> . . . For all of them are adulterers, a band of cheaters.
> They have spanned their bow, the tongue.
> Falsehood and not faithfulness prevails in the land,
> For they have gone from wrong to wrong
> And do not know me, God says.
> Be on your guard against each other
> And do not trust even a brother,
> For every brother acts most treacherously
> And every comrade is a talebearer.
> Their tongue is a fatal arrow:

With the mouth one speaks deceit;
One says "Peace" to one's companion
But inwardly lies in wait for him.
They scoff at each other
And do not speak honestly.
They have trained their tongue to speak falsehood;
They have strayed and can no more return.
Abuse upon abuse, deceit upon deceit;
They have refused to know me, God says (9:1b-3, 7, 4 f.).[14]

Failure to know God is an act of unfaithfulness, the equivalent of rebellion:

The priests did not say: "Where is God?"
They that handle the law did not know me.
The shepherds rebelled;
The prophets prophesied for Baal,
Pursued futilities (2:8).

It is a kind of foolishness:

For my people are foolish,
They do not know me.
They are stupid children,
They lack understanding.
They are skilled in wrongdoing,
Know not how to do right (4:22).

In search of just and faithful men Jeremiah considered the poor and the rich but found in both classes folly combined with the lack of knowledge of God's way.

I said: "But [these are] the poor;
They act foolishly

[14] Omitting a preposition in verse 2a and reading a verb as singular; reading verse 7 after verse 3 and with a different word division in verse 5.

> Because they do not know God's way,
> The requirements of their Lord.
> Let me go to the great
> And speak with them.
> Surely they know God's way,
> The requirements of their Lord."
> But they as well had cast off the yoke,
> Broken all bonds (5:4 f.).

He compared his people to the lower animals, but to his people's disadvantage:

> Even the stork in the heavens
> Knows her appointed seasons;
> The dove and the swift and the bulbul
> Return at their proper times.
> But my people do not know
> The requirements of God (8:7).

Jeremiah twice explicitly defined knowledge of God. Once, having set it up as the highest of all human values, he described it as man's imitation in human society of God's way with man. Even as God displays the qualities of constancy, justice, and righteousness, so he desires these qualities in man. To assent to this is to know God.

> Let the wise man not boast of his wisdom,
> Let the strong man not boast of his strength,
> Let the rich man not boast of his riches;
> But of this let him boast who boasts:
> That he understands and knows me,
> That I, God, act on earth
> With constancy, justice and righteousness—
> That I desire these [qualities], God says (9:22 f.).

The second definition appears within a rebuke which Jeremiah addressed to the king, Jehoiakim. He compared Jehoiakim with his father the king, Josiah. The son had certain tastes and interests, but knowledge of God was found in the father, the justice of whose rule was as natural for him as eating and drinking.

> Do you prove yourself king by surpassing in cedar wood?
> Did not your father eat and drink
> And act with justice and righteousness . . . ?
> He heard the cause of the poor and needy . . .
> Is this not knowledge of me? God says (22:15 f.).

Other (false) prophets were small help in the matter of implanting the knowledge of God in the hearts of men. Those prophets, whether in Samaria or Jerusalem, could not guide the people aright by instruction, much less by example. They themselves did not know God, for they had not stood near him. And as for serving as examples, they so offended by their own behavior that they seemed rather to abet the other malefactors.

> And among Samaria's prophets
> I observed an unseemly thing:
> They prophesied by Baal
> And led my people Israel astray.
> And among Jerusalem's prophets
> I observed a horrible thing:
> They themselves engaged in adultery and false dealing,
> And they reassured the wrongdoers
> So that no one turned from his wrong.
> They all became to me like Sodom,
> And [Jerusalem's] inhabitants like those of Gomorrah
>   (23:13 f.).

> If they stood in my council
> They would then tell my people my words
> And deflect them from their evil way
> And their wrongdoings (23:22).

And so, according to Jeremiah, a people's knowledge of God expresses itself in terms of a harmonious society. Men who know God act with justice and integrity; and when, in other contexts, through Jeremiah God demands such conduct he is simply asking such knowledge. So, for example, in the "temple sermon," already quoted:[15]

> . . . Promote justice between man and man, do not oppress stranger, orphan or widow . . . and do not go after other gods to your hurt . . . Lo, you depend on profitless delusions. Will you steal, kill, engage in adultery, swear to falsehood, sacrifice to Baal, and go after other gods . . . and come and stand before me in this house . . . and say: We are safe? (7:5 f., 8-10).

And also, for example, in the charge to the royal house:

> . . . Promote justice and righteousness, deliver the robbed from oppression's hand, wrong no stranger, orphan, or widow, do no violence, spill no innocent blood in this place (22:3).

These are only extensions of Jeremiah's definition of knowledge of God.

And when, under the influence of Jeremiah, a later prophet thought of the ideal society of the future, as shall yet appear,[16] he thought of a society where knowledge of God is universal, inscribed on every heart.

[15] See above, p. 10.
[16] See below, pp. 210 f. on 31:34 and compare 24:7.

But can knowledge of God be written down in a book? How is the knowledge which Jeremiah commended related to biblical law? Jeremiah was a contemporary of the king Josiah, and as such he lived through the reformation which Josiah sponsored in 621, his eighteenth year.[17] If, as still seems most probable, the book which Hilkiah the priest found in the temple at that time and which shaped the program of that reform was the canonical book of Deuteronomy or an essential segment of Deuteronomy, then we would expect to find in Jeremiah some references to its royal sponsor and its laws. And quite possibly there are a few such references.

In the first place, there is the paragraph just cited in praise of Josiah, notable for its succinct definition of knowledge of God (22:15 f.). Josiah knew how to live. Then there are a few specific allusions to deuteronomic legislation. In the temple sermon Jeremiah quoted the "ten commandments" of Deut. 5 (though, of course, these appear likewise in Exod. 20). More particularly, in 3:1 he alludes to the law concerning divorce which stands in Deut. 24:1-4, and in 34:14 he quotes the law specifying the rights of Hebrew slaves, not that releasing male slaves only, in Exod. 21:2-11, but the one in Deut. 15:12-18.[18]

And there are two passages in which Jeremiah seems to pass judgment on the reform as a whole. One of these refers to Judah with the symbolic name Bagodah ("perfidious"):

Yet in spite of all this, Bagodah, her sister Judah, did not come back to me with her whole heart, but only in bad faith, God says (3:10).

[17] See II Kings 22:3-23:25.
[18] See above, pp. 14, 182, and 47, n. 1.

The reference is not specific, yet it seems to speak of a reform in Judah; Judah did "come back" to God—though "in bad faith"—not "with her whole heart." This half-hearted reform may have been Josiah's. If in this one passage Jeremiah hesitantly approves the deuteronomic legislation, in the second passage he emphatically denounces it:

How can you say: "We are wise,
And with us is the law of God"?
Lo, surely, it has wrought falsehood—
That false pen of the scribes (8:8).

These "scribes" are probably to be identified with them "that handle the law" in an earlier passage: "The priests did not say: 'Where is God?' They that handle the law did not know me" (2:8). Here the "law" (*torah*) is quite possibly the deuteronomic legislation, and if so, then Jeremiah here withdraws his tentative endorsement.

It is perhaps strange that Jeremiah refers so seldom to Josiah's reform. On the other hand, if his opinion was as unfavorable as these latter passages suggest, it becomes quite possible that a deuteronomic editor of Jeremiah's book, jealous for the deuteronomic position, simply eliminated other such expressions. Jeremiah's book appears, indeed, to have experienced a deuteronomic redaction; there are several added paragraphs written in the language of Deuteronomy, one of which even seems designed to make Jeremiah advertise the deuteronomic reform (see the Fourth Additional Note, p. 243). But though he might have hesitated Jeremiah seems not to have endorsed the program in the end.

There are aspects of that legislation which might have

appealed to Jeremiah. It had a concern, even as he did,
for the poor, the stranger, the widow, and the orphan—
for justice too.[19] It even contained his exhortation touching
the uncircumcised heart.

> Circumcise the foreskin of your heart and be stiffnecked no
> more (Deut. 10:16).[20]

And even as Jeremiah, Deuteronomy expressed a primary
concern for exclusive devotion to God, undiluted by service to Baal or other strange gods.[21]

But there is another essential feature of the law in Deuteronomy, which Jeremiah would have found disappoint-
ing, or indeed wholly unacceptable. The pervasive and
dominant theme in Deuteronomy—that Jerusalem is the
city which God has chosen for his residence, for his "name"
to dwell there [22]—is completely at variance with the
prophet's insistence that Jerusalem is vulnerable and
doomed. The vulnerability of Jerusalem and the folly of
believing that the temple is a fortress and high tower, "the
stronghold in which you take pride" (Ezek. 24:21), are
the whole point of Jeremiah's "temple sermon" in chapter
7, and Jeremiah predicts there that Jerusalem will fare
like Shiloh (7:14) although he must know that this assault
upon the incontestable primacy of Jerusalem could cost
him his life.[23] Even after his narrow escape he insists that
the vessels left in the house after the first looting will yet

[19] Compare Jer. 7:5 f., 9 and p. 13, above, with Deut. 16:11 f.; 24:10-
15, 17-19; and Jer. 22:3 with Deut. 16:18-20 et passim.
[20] Compare Jer. 4:4 and pp. 193-96, below.
[21] Compare the passages quoted above on pp. 178-82 with Deut.
12:2 f., 30 f.; 16:21 et passim.
[22] Deut. 12:5, 14, and often.
[23] See Chapter I, above.

be carried away,[24] and repeatedly he says that the house
will be ruined and desolate, and that God will give Zion
into the hands of the king of Babylon, who will reduce
it to ashes.[25]

One wonders to what extent Jeremiah is here battling
the Jerusalem priesthood now newly entrenched behind
the laws of Deuteronomy. Surely if at all, then to a limited
extent only, because he had other reasons for believing
that Jerusalem must fall.

However that may be, Jeremiah did not depend upon
"the law" as the force which would instill loyalty and the
knowledge of God into the hearts of the men of Judah.

These were among the thoughts that dominated Jeremiah's prophetic ministry: that God demands of his people
loyalty, faithfulness, devotion to him alone, and that their
leaving him for other gods is a fatal error; that nevertheless God can recognize amendment—amendment in the
shape of "knowledge of God," and expressed in terms of
a harmonious society—and that therefore reconciliation is
at least conceivable.

But Jeremiah seems not to have put much faith in any
program of reform such as Josiah's Deuteronomy—seems
rather to have hoped for something less external than a
written code. It was his hope, his vain hope, that he might
reach the "heart" of his people.

[24] See Jer. 27:17-22.
[25] See Jer. 9:10; 22:5; 21:10; 38:3 et passim.

XIII

The Uncircumcised Heart,
Discipline, and the Foe
from the North

The symbol of Jeremiah's frustration is the "uncircumcised heart." Since biblical psychology localizes feelings and emotions in the viscera and looks to the heart as the organ of comprehension, an uncircumcised heart is "a closed mind." Jeremiah had undertaken to plant knowledge in the mind of his people and his phrase "uncircumcised heart" was his admission of defeat. In an earlier century Isaiah too had spoken with bitter irony of the heart made fat, too gross for understanding, like veiled eyes and stopped ears.[1] Angry, Jeremiah combined invective with colorful language to name the closed mind. The insensitive, the impermeable, the wilfully closed mind was for Jeremiah "the uncircumcised heart."

When Jeremiah first uses the figure he makes quite clear both his meaning and his mood. An analogy defines his phrase, and a threat reveals his mood. His analogy has to do with farming. A farmer does not plant an untilled

[1] Isa. 6:10.

land which weeds have taken over. To make the soil productive, first he ploughs it and rids it of weeds. So it is
with man; the human mind as well must be cleared of
noxious growth and made receptive. Only then can ideas
strike root and grow. This is the obvious meaning of the
figure in its first appearance: the uncircumcised heart is
the unreceptive mind.

> For so God said to the men of Judah and to Jerusalem:
> Plough your unploughed ground
> And do not sow among thorns.
> Be circumcised to me [2]
> And remove the foreskins of your heart,
> O men of Judah and inhabitants of Jerusalem,
> Lest my wrath break out like fire
> And burn with none to quench it,
> Because of your evil deeds (4:3-4).

The idea, quite explicit in this first passage, occurs again
in 9:25: ". . . all the house of Israel are uncircumcised
of heart." And the ear being portal to the mind, "the
uncircumcised ear" is only a variant of the same thought:

> To whom can I speak and testify and be heard?
> Lo, their ear is uncircumcised and they can not listen . . .
>   (6:10).

The mind can be rigid or the mind can be open and flexi-
ble; so the prophets can speak of a "heart of stone" and
equally of a "heart of flesh." In the words of Ezekiel,
God said: "I shall remove from your body the heart of

---

[2] Reading "to me" and not "to God," since God is speaking. A presumed abbreviation was mistakenly resolved.

stone and give you a heart of flesh" (36:26b). Habits are
like grooves in the mind, they are ineradicable on a heart
of stone. That appears to be Jeremiah's meaning in 17:1:

> The guilt of Judah is incised with an iron pen,
> Engraved with a diamond point on the tablet of their
>   heart . . .

This same quasi deterministic sentiment appears again in
the proverbial irony of 13:23:

> Can an Ethiopian change his skin or a leopard his spots?
> So little can you improve who are schooled in evil.

Similarly the question in 8:5 is an expression of despair:

> Why is this people wayward
> . . . Persistently astray?
> They have held firmly to deceit,
> Have refused to come back.

But in Jeremiah this species of determinism must come
to terms with a freedom of human choice. In the following
passage God does not initiate the action; it is "they" who
stubbornly refuse, and so themselves invite disaster:

> . . . Because they made their necks stiff so as not to hear
>   my words
> I shall do to this city and to all her villages the whole evil
>   that I have threatened to do her (19:15).

Equally well, if only they were animated by a resolute
will, they could wash the not so indelible wickedness from
their heart:

Wash away the evil from your heart, O Jerusalem, that you
may be saved.
How long shall wicked thoughts abide within you? (4:14).

Indeed, this freedom was a feature in the first cited refer-
ance to the uncircumcised heart. The plea addressed to
Jerusalem here ("Wash away the evil from your heart")
is a variant of the appeal earlier in the same chapter:
"Remove the foreskins of your heart, O men of Judah,"
and of the frequent summons to "return." [3]

Jeremiah found it almost impossible to "get through"
to the minds of his people. Prophets recognized two
means of communication from God to people, and Jeremiah found neither effective. The one was through prophets like himself by way of the spoken word. The other
was through interpreted experience, the learning done
in suffering. The one was "the word of God," the other
was *musar*, "discipline." A rabbinic interpretation of
Haggai 1:12 made reference to these two modes. The
verse says of Zerubbabel, Joshua, and the remnant of
the people that they "listened to the voice of the Lord
their God and to the words of Haggai the prophet." For
the thirteenth-century rabbinic exegete David Ḳimḥi,
the word "and" between "the voice of the Lord" and "the
words of Haggai" needed explaining; for were the words
of Haggai not indeed the voice of God? Exploiting the
conjunction, the exegete discovered in the verse the two
modes of divine instruction; he differentiated between the
words of the prophet and the voice of God, the voice of
God being the historical process in which the perceptive
may see arguments as compelling as any advanced by
God's prophets. Valid or not as an interpretation of the

[3] See above, pp. 26 and 182 f.

passage in Haggai, this exegesis directs the attention to that kind of revelation which Jeremiah called *musar*.

It is a fairly frequent idea in Jeremiah and the meaning of the word is usually transparent. *Musar* is discipline, suffering imposed with a design, pain inflicted for a purpose, calculated to produce amendment.

To no avail I smote your sons [God says],
They did not accept *musar* . . . (2:30).

Lord, do you not look for faithfulness? [the prophet asks].
You smote them and they did not feel hurt;
You brought destruction on them; they refused to accept *musar.*
They set their faces harder than stone;
They refused to come back (5:3).

. . . This is the people that did not listen to the voice of the Lord their God and did not accept *musar;* faithfulness has given out and is lacking in their speech (7:28).

. . . I bereaved, I destroyed my people;
They did not turn back from their ways (15:7b).

Jeremiah urged his people to take a lesson from their defeat:

The evil that has befallen you should teach you;
The reverses you have suffered should admonish you.
Apprehend and be aware that wrong and bitter
Was your abandoning the Lord your God . . . (2:19).

The Hebrew word translated "teach" at the beginning of this passage is a form of the verb from which *musar* is derived. A form of the verb or noun occurs in several other passages. Among them are an appeal, a backward glance at a disciplinary act of unusual severity, and a response which ideally such discipline might evoke. First, the appeal:

> Accept discipline, O Jerusalem,
> Or I must loathe you;
> Or I must make you a desolate,
> Uninhabited land (6:8).

Next, the backward glance:

> . . . I struck you as an enemy strikes,
> With a cruel man's discipline . . . (30:14b).

Finally, the fancied, desired response:

> . . . "You disciplined me and I accepted discipline
> [Who had been] like an untrained calf.
> Now take me and let me come back,
> For you are the Lord my God" (31:18).

As a rule the discipline, the evil, the reverses are in the field of battle, defeat, slaughter, captivity. But God also disciplines men with the forces of nature. A drought is an "act of God":

> The dew was withheld,
> The latter rains did not come,
> But you had the forehead of a harlot,
> You refused to know humiliation (3:3).

A related thought is less evident, but is not wholly absent from Jeremiah, the thought that God also tries with love to reach the "heart" of his people. What discipline could not achieve the gifts of love might yet accomplish. A later prophet, Zechariah, seems to have had this thought in mind when (in 8:14-17) he let an exhortation to virtuous living follow upon a promise of divine favor. That God wooed his recalcitrant bride with lavish generosity but all in vain appears to be the sense of a passage in Jeremiah's third chapter.

> I thought: How I will set you up among sons
> And give you a land of delight,
> As possession a beauty of beauties of nations!
> And I thought: You will call me "My father!"
> And will not stray from me.
> But as a wife betrays her companion
> You betrayed me, O house of Israel, God says (3:19 f.).

Love too had failed.

Neither through his prophets by word nor directly through deed, to deter or to entice, could God reach the uncircumcised heart of his people. What Jeremiah said did not disturb them; they simply did not hear it. God's *musar*, too, was wasted on them; they were inert.

And yet probably Jeremiah's public was no more obdurate than a cross section of humankind. Prophetic invective can be misleading, and closed minds are characteristic of no single people in no single age. His contemporaries had no monopoly on those obstacles to communication which thwarted Jeremiah. Any man trying to say to any people what Jeremiah came to say would meet with his discouragement. For Jeremiah came to say that greed was wrong and that all was not well; he came to disturb those that were at ease in Zion.

If disturbing the peace was a misdemeanor in Bible times Jeremiah was surely an offender. Not indeed with

malice, yet with premeditation he undertook to disturb
the peace of the people of Judah. Jeremiah sensed the
approach of disaster and sounded an alarm. He declared
that an enemy, drawing inexorably nearer, was menacing
the land—that invasion with its wake of pillage, slaughter,
and captivity, was imminent. He screamed the doom, but
with small effect.

He spoke at first, naming no names, of "a foe from
the north," and his visions of the enemy's advance and the
consternation of the defenders are graphic and dramatic.
There are a number of such descriptions [4] and this is a
sampling of them:

> Tell it in Judah,
> Proclaim it in Jerusalem . . .
> Sound the alarm in the land,
> Call loudly and say:
> "Assemble and let us enter
> The fortified cities."
> Set up a marker: "To Zion";
> Take refuge without delay.

> [*Now God is speaking:*]

> For I am bringing calamity from the north,
> Great havoc.
> The lion has set out from his covert,
> The destroyer of nations is on the march—has left his place—
> To make your land a desolation,
> Your cities to be uninhabited ruins (4:5-7).

> Lo! like clouds he goes,
> His chariots are like a tempest,

---

[4] Jer. 1:13-16; 4:5-31; 5:15-17; 6:1-8, 22-26; 8:14-16; related are
10:17-22 and 13:20-22.

His horses are swifter than eagles.
"Woe unto us, we are undone!" (4:13).

Ah, my inward parts! I writhe.
Ah, the walls of my heart!
I am deeply disturbed,
I can not keep still,
For I have heard the sound of alarm,
The cry of war.
Breaking follows on breaking,
All the land is ruined.
Suddenly my tent is ruined,
On an instant my tent curtains.
How much longer must I see the standards,
Hear the alarm? (4:19-21).

Unto [Zion] shepherds come,
With their flocks.
They have encamped about her,
They are feeding where they are.

[*The hostile shepherd-kings speak:*]

"Prepare war upon her.
Arise and we will go up at high noon.
Alas, that the day declines,
That the shadows of evening grow long!
Arise and we will go up at night,
And we will destroy her towers . . .
Cut down trees;
Raise siegeworks against Jerusalem" (6:3-6a).

[*Zion speaks of the foe:*]

"We have heard of him;
Our hands grow weak.

Pangs take hold of us
Like the pain of a woman in childbirth."

Go not into the field,
Walk not on the way,
For the enemy [is there] with sword,
Terror round about.
Dress in sackcloth, O daughter of my people,
Roll in ashes.
Mourn as for an only son,
With bitter lamentation.

"For suddenly has come
The destroyer upon us" (6:24-26).

Nearly always, in Judah, invasions came from the north.
Although on the map Assyria and Babylonia lie more east
than north of Jerusalem, by the time their armies reached
Palestine they were coming down from the north. So the
fact that the unnamed foe in these passages would approach "from the north" fails to identify him, but it is
not necessary to look for any mystery people out of the
north land to play the role of God's weapon according
to Jeremiah. Whether for Jeremiah that rod of God's
wrath was Assyria, experiencing the decline that led in
612 to the fall of Nineveh, or was Babylonia, the rising
Mesopotamian power which by 605 was extending its
empire energetically westward, Jeremiah probably had
in mind no other than the currently powerful state "between the two rivers."

The fact that, in the latter years of Josiah, Assyria was
in reality fighting for its own survival with no time to
take care of God's affairs would not have hindered Jeremiah in thinking that danger for Judah could come from

that quarter. Consider the analogous situation in the time of Amos. It was still some years before Tiglath Pileser's restoration of Assyria's fortunes when Amos predicted Assyria's conquest of Ephraim and the exile of the complacent inhabitants of Samaria to that place "beyond Damascus" (Amos 5:27). To be sure, Amos did not designate Assyria by name—in that respect, too, the form of his prediction foreshadowed that of Jeremiah's; Amos merely said: "For lo! I will bring up against you, O house of Israel, says the Lord God of hosts, a nation" (6:14). Amos spoke of "a nation" (*goy*), content to use the general term and leave such a phrase as "beyond Damascus" (in 5:27) to suggest the particular—the less crucial particular. It remained for Isaiah to call on the name of Assyria and to confer upon that nation (in Isaiah's day fast expanding westward and with Judah in its path) the title: "rod of [God's] wrath" (Isa. 10:5). Zephaniah clearly located Assyria in "the north" (Zeph. 2:13).

Jeremiah's predictions were both general, like those of Amos, and particular, like those of Isaiah. Again and again Jeremiah spoke vaguely of "the kingdoms of the north" (1:15), of a *goy*, "a nation from afar" (5:15), an *'am*, "a people coming from a country of the north, a great nation aroused from the far parts of the earth" (6:22); and with equal frequency he spoke of Babylonia and of its conquering sovereign, Nebuchadrezzar, specifically and by name. Not impossibly it was while the political situation in Mesopotamia was confused that Jeremiah spoke indefinitely, like Amos, of the foe from the north. However that may be, after Babylonia had become the undisputed master of the land between the rivers and the westward march of empire moved unchecked, Jeremiah, like Isaiah, could and did specify the agent of Judah's doom.

Jeremiah's biographer made record of many such words. The first dated reference to Babylonia appears in the preface to the copy of the scroll which Baruch prepared after Jehoiakim had burned the original. That was at about 605–4, just when Jeremiah might be expected to become specific.[5] Then God said: "I am about to take all the tribes of the north . . . and my servant Nebuchadrezzar, king of Babylon, and bring them in against this land and its people . . ." (25:9).[6] Some years later, around 594, Jeremiah acted out his convictions by wearing a yoke, the symbol of Babylon's supremacy, and urging a like course upon his king: "And I said to Zedekiah, king of Judah . . . Bring your neck under the yoke of Babylon's king and serve him and his people and live" (27:12). When Hananiah took violent issue with him, that encounter only strengthened Jeremiah's conviction: "You have broken bars of wood," he said, "only to make way for bars of iron" (28:13). Twice more Jeremiah spoke to Zedekiah predicting a Babylonian victory: "And after that, God says, I will give Zedekiah, king of Judah, and his servants . . . over to Nebuchadrezzar . . . and he will put them to the sword without mercy, without pity, without compassion" (21:7). A second time, in answer to the king's question, "Is there a word from God?" he said: "There is. You will fall into the hands of the king of Babylon" (37:17). And in Jerusalem's last days he drove home his certainty with grim and emphatic reiteration: "If you had smitten all the army of the Chaldaeans

---

[5] Concerning the dates in this paragraph, see J. P. Hyatt, "New Light on Nebuchadrezzar and Judean History" in *JBL*, LXXV (1956), 280 f.
[6] See above, pp. 31 f.

who are warring with you and only wounded men were left of them, they would arise, each in his tent, and burn this city" (37:10). "I am handing this city over to Babylon's king and he will destroy it by fire" (34:2). "If you fight the Chaldaeans you will not succeed" (32:5).[7] So if in his earlier years Jeremiah spoke somewhat vaguely about a foe from the north he was quite specific in his latter years about the foe's identity.

There are other possible answers,[8] but this is the probable one: that the unnamed northern adversary and the oft-named Babylonia are only variants of the one conception—that by a northern route from the land between the rivers the people would come whom God had summoned for his purpose towards Israel.

Men do not relish being disturbed. The accustomed is the comfortable; the always believed is the congenial; and "what I don't know doesn't hurt me." Jeremiah found communication difficult. Exhortation beat helplessly on the closed mind, the uncircumcised heart; *musar*, God-sent discipline, went unheeded; and even threats proved futile. Jeremiah's experience with his people taught him that he could not frighten them into virtue.

> I spoke to you in your languid ease;
> You said: "I will not listen" (22:21).

Jeremiah had "mingled" and the impressions which he had gathered induced despair. In the society which he had come to know it seemed that just and faithful men were simply lacking.

---

[7] See above, pp. 39-45, 50, 52 f.
[8] On this question see Hyatt, *op. cit.*, p. 283 f.

Roam the streets of Jerusalem,
Observe and learn;
Search well its thoroughfares
To discover a man—
If there be one—who pursues justice,
Who desires faithfulness . . . (5:1).

Jeremiah knew also what word was in everyone's mouth.
The slogan of his day was "Peace," *shalom.*

Small and great, all pursue gain;
Prophet or priest, all play false,
And they have found a cure for the impending ruin of my
     people
All too lightly, in that they say: "Peace, peace!"
Though peace is lacking (6:13 f.).

The beautiful word was an incantation; saying "Peace"—
saying it over and over—produced peace—or, at any rate,
the illusion of peace.

A chorus of prophets said: "You will have peace"
(4:10). "Who can descend upon us? Who can enter our
sheltering places?" (21:13). "God has said: You will have
peace . . . No harm will befall you" (23:17). "You will
not experience war; there will be no want; I will provide
sure peace in this place" (14:13). "No war or want in
this land!" (14:15). These were the prophets whom the
people believed, these sounding boards for their own wish-
thoughts.

The prophets prophesy in the service of falsehood,
And the priests bear rule at their side,
And my people want it to be so . . . (5:31).

Other prophets—Jeremiah, Uriah among them—went unheeded, but these were believed. Of such forebodings as Jeremiah uttered, the people said—for they could charm away an evil by denying it:

". . . It is not so.
And no harm will befall us,
And we shall not experience war or want.
And the prophets [the Jeremiahs] are wind;
They do not have the [authentic] word . . ." (5:12 f.).

Jeremiah spoke of the difference between prophets and prophets, those like himself who "prophesied . . . of war, disaster, and disease" and the prophet "who prophesies good" (28:8 f.).[9] And Jeremiah knew which of them enjoyed acclaim. The people heard the words of the prophets who prophesied "good." But however loudly Jeremiah protested, the people could not hear him—and scarcely a ripple disturbed their bog.

What room was there, then, for hope?

[9] See above, p. 40.

XIV

The Shape of Jeremiah's Hope

In the matter of hope Jeremiah differed from Amos and the first Isaiah. According to Amos the eschatological "day" which God had in readiness for his people was a day of darkness and not light; and still for Isaiah it was a day of irretrievable national defeat, as final as death. Isaiah thought his people's plight to be utterly desperate; Isaiah admitted no conscious hope.[1] But Jeremiah did. Despite his distressing certainty that his insensate people was doomed Jeremiah cherished a hope. Unlike Amos and the first Isaiah, Jeremiah consciously cherished and not infrequently gave expression to a hope for a future for his people.

Two aspects of hope appear in the book of Jeremiah, but they do not lay equal claim to authenticity. The one better known is probably not original with the prophet Jeremiah; it is only, with a measure of plausibility, attributed to him. It is what we call "the new covenant." Although the conception so designated is a notable contribution to prophetic religion, the chances are great that

[1] See Blank, "Traces of Prophetic Agony in Isaiah," *HUCA*, XXVII (1956), 86-90.

a prophet other than Jeremiah, a person familiar with
Jeremiah's manner but not wholly imbued with his spirit,
and probably living quite a bit later than he, was the
real author of the "new covenant" paragraph.

The prophetic author of the passage phrased the expectation that a future age would see accomplished all
that Jeremiah had failed to achieve, outfaced as he was
by stubborn disbelievers. To the three means which God
and his human agents could conceivably employ in an
effort to reclaim the doomed nation the new-covenant
writer added a fourth. The first three methods had failed.
The one direct method did not succeed: a thick-skinned
people had not yielded to the persuasion of *musar;* to no
avail God had laid on them the disciplinary rod of hard
experience.[2] Nor had either of the mediated forms of
schooling produced desired results; neither through legis-
lators nor through prophets had God been able to communicate with his people. As for the one, "the false pen
of the scribes" had only "wrought falsehood" and Judah
had not come back "with her whole heart, but only in
bad faith."[3] As for the other, Jeremiah had come to the
anguishing realization that this people, "all the house of
Israel," was "uncircumcised of heart";[4] Jeremiah could
see no means whereby such a prophet as he could get
through to the hearts, the minds, of his people. It was
probably these considerations which suggested to some
spiritual heir of the prophet Jeremiah the "new covenant."
This heir of Jeremiah substituted for the unavailing measures a fourth—a measure which by its nature simply could
not fail to assure the regeneration of a people. God, he

[2] See above, pp. 196-99.
[3] Jer. 8:8; 3:10; see above, pp. 189 f.
[4] Jer. 9:25; see above, pp. 193-96.

said, would remake the house of Israel; he would implant
the knowledge of him in every heart. That is the new
covenant which at some future time God would make
with his people—in days to come.

> Lo! days will come, God says, when I will establish with
> Israel and Judah a new covenant, not like the covenant
> which I established with their fathers when I took them by
> the hand to bring them from Egypt's land, which covenant
> they broke although I was master to them, God says. For
> this is the covenant which I will establish with Israel after
> those days, God says: I will put my law in their inward
> parts and will write it on their heart, and I will be their
> God and they will be my people, and they will not need
> to teach any more each his fellow and each his brother,
> saying: "Know God!" for they will all know me from the
> least of them to the greatest, God says, for I will pardon
> their guilt and no more remember their sin (31:31-34).

This new covenant is both like and unlike Jeremiah.
Two features characteristic of Jeremiah here combine
with an element less familiar, one that appears less congenial and suggests the work of a different hand. The
opened heart and the new-found individual suggest the
prophet Jeremiah; not so the divine determinism. This
last was not Jeremiah's pattern.

The passage reads as though designed to relieve Jeremiah's distress at the uncircumcised heart, the impermeable mind, the character incised as by an iron pen with
guilt. Although Jeremiah had repeatedly asked to be
heard, although he had exhorted his people continually to
"return," confronted by their consistent refusal he was
tortured with the suspicion that they could not return,
that they could not even hear, that their minds were

totally unimpressionable. It is this condition which the new covenant would rectify—with a single stroke, so to speak. What the new covenant would achieve would, in this respect, be the consummation of Jeremiah's unending labors. On the now-opened hearts of his people, in place of the guilt once written there, knowledge of God would be indelibly inscribed.

Not that alone, but this knowledge would now be written on the heart of each member of the house of Israel, each one "from the least of them to the greatest," with the consequence that no one would need to instruct any other—that there would be no longer any need for prophets. Also this feature of the new covenant reads like an extension of a Jeremianic tendency. For in Jeremiah the individual was emerging. Within the mass Jeremiah had been able to distinguish and recognize men deserving by reason of the quality of their spirit. Jeremiah could single out from the community a faithful Baruch, his friend who shared his lot as fugitive, or a trusting Eved-melech, the Ethiopian officer who rescued him from the pit, or loyal Rechabites for their demonstrated constancy —Jeremiah could single them out and promise them personal survival in a unitary national disaster. Jeremiah's recognition of men's virtue, his thinking in terms of individual merit, his rewarding of deserving persons, was no doubt the fruit of his own inner experience. His assumption, too, that others could attain to knowledge of God was certainly the externalization of his immediate personal experience of God. This eminently introspective prophet went so very far on the road to a "personal religion" that it is not strange to find here attributed to him a notable expression of personal religion.

Jeremiah could himself have taken these two steps: he

could have fancied the knowledge of God lodged at last
in all obdurate hearts, and he could have gone on from
his personal experience to an ultimate expression of personal religion. In these two features Jeremiah had himself moved in the direction of the new covenant formula.
And were there no negative indications he might pass
as its author. One who firmly insists that Jeremiah did
in fact write the passage will not be convinced by the
argument against his authorship which here follows, for
it only tips the balance against that view. And this much
must surely be said: that the true author of the passage
stood under the influence of Jeremiah and knew well why
he ascribed it to this one among the prophets instead of
another.

But there is reason to doubt that Jeremiah went the
whole way to the new covenant and took also the third
step; the determinism which characterizes the concept is
not congenial to the prophet Jeremiah. The author of
the new covenant passage tacitly deprives his people of
all initiative and so, of all responsibility. It is God, he
says, who will establish the new relationship, who will
forgive all sins and put his law in the inward parts of his
people—making that knowledge an inherent human trait,
like reflexes and like natural instincts—and writing it on
each single separate heart. This covenant is an act of
grace, and as such it is, except for one ambiguous possibility, unmatched in Jeremiah. There is, to be sure,
that one brief word in 24:7: "And I will give them a heart
to know me . . ."; but that is all, and even here the conclusion of the same verse introduces confusion: ". . . if
[or when] they return [?], [or because they will return
?], to me with their whole heart"—as though it were
conditional grace. The divine determinism in the new

covenant passage is so little like Jeremiah's pattern that it casts strong doubt on his presumed authorship of the paragraph.

Jeremiah does not otherwise refer to the new covenant.[5] In fact, it is hardly attested elsewhere in the Bible. Ezekiel approaches the thought, for example in 36:25-27: ". . . I will give you a new heart, and a new spirit I will put within you, and I will remove the heart of stone from your body and give you a heart of flesh. . . ." But there is silence otherwise. If Jeremiah had really been the author of the fertile concept it would hardly have received so little notice during the centuries following, while yet the Hebrew canon was taking shape. It is probably, therefore, the product of a considerably later stage in the unfolding of biblical thought. The language also points in that direction. The expressions have a messianic or utopian character: "Days will come"; it will happen "after those days." This is not the usual language of Jeremiah who consistently speaks in terms not of eschatology but of organic history. Elsewhere in Jeremiah's book his hope for Israel's future is set in a different frame.

Jeremiah's hope had a bite to it. It was hope for a rebuilding after the collapse of the nation, for a replanting after an uprooting. This was the sense of Jeremiah's first understanding of his mission: he was sent, so he reported, "to root out and tear down, and to lay waste and destroy" and after that "to rebuild and to replant" (1:10).[6] Jerusalem, he knew, must be destroyed before it could be newly built; the men of Judah must be torn from their

[5] On Jer. 32:40; 33:8 and the rest of Jer. 33, see Fourth Additional Note, pp. 243 f.

[6] See above, p. 73.

soil before they could be gathered to their land again; his people's tomorrow would not dawn before a night had passed.

Why Jeremiah thought in this fashion has yet to be considered; that he thought so is apparent in a number of passages, only a few of which have been reviewed as yet. His graphic demonstration of hope in chapter 32, where, though he foresaw Jerusalem's imminent destruction, he yet bought a field, contains the significant supplementary information that he took pains to preserve the record of this purchase in his kind of safety vault for the distant future,[7] evidence that he hoped for a restoration only after a calamity, and not too soon thereafter.

When the blow had fallen and exiles of 587 had joined exiles of 598, when, then, conspirators among the remnant in the land had murdered Gedaliah, and when the ultimate survivors, ready to flee to Egypt for sanctuary, consulted Jeremiah he pondered for ten days and then returned God's reassuring word to them:

> If you will only dwell in this land I shall rebuild you and not destroy you and I shall plant and not uproot you [again], for I am sorry for the blow I dealt you. Do not fear the king of Babylon whom you fear. Do not fear him, God says, for I am with you to save and deliver you from his power. And I will secure compassion for you and he will have compassion on you and restore you to your land (42:10-12).[8]

Here again, as in chapter 32, a beginning follows an end, and it is because the worst has happened that Jeremiah can speak of a better.

The lesson that Jeremiah derived (in 18:1-6) from

[7] See above, pp. 56 f.
[8] See above, pp. 58 f.

what he saw in the potter's workshop had similar import; it, too, was hope. And he may have written that lesson at some time after the fall of Jerusalem in 587 or even after the subsequent murder of Gedaliah. The passage is undated and no internal evidence suggests a date. One can only observe that his message here was peculiarly suited for such a situation as that in which the Judean remnant found itself after 587, or at the time of the flight to Egypt. It urges hope upon the hopeless: You must believe, it says, that God can help. The point of Jeremiah's analogy is not immediately apparent. It has been obscured by the addition of vv. 7 to 11, an unrelated composition with a different purpose.[9] A misinterpretation is facilitated also by the fact that the word *nishhat*, "spoiled" (here in Jer. 18:4), has two meanings both in Hebrew and in English. It can mean "corrupted morally"—as it does in the story of the flood (Gen. 6:11), or it can mean "damaged" or "ruined"—as it does in Jeremiah's story of the loincloth (Jer. 13:7).[10] But it is in this latter sense that Jeremiah here employs the term; the analogy is between the marred vessel in the hand of the potter and the ravaged land. What Jeremiah observed in the potter's workshop was the ease with which the potter working with wet clay could make over a vessel which he had spoiled, ruined: "Whenever the vessel which he was making of the clay in the potter's hand was spoiled he would start again and make of it another vessel, as it pleased the potter to do" (v. 4). The potter could repair the damage which he had done. What Jeremiah then learned through a word from God, was God's competence to do the same for Israel: "Am I not able to do to you, O house of Israel, as this

[9] It is an exhortation similar in import to Ezek. 18:21-23.
[10] See above, p. 181.

potter does? God says. You are in my hand, O house of
Israel, like the clay in the potter's hand" (v. 6). The
"spoiled" vessel of the potter symbolizes the people, with
land desolate, capital city in ruins, sanctuary in ashes—
spoiled. And the symbol is a reassurance, an encouragement. It may well have been a much needed lesson. It is
indeed probable that the survivors after Gedaliah, sea-
soned by prophetic word and recurrent crushing defeat,
found it then as hard to hope for safety as formerly to
believe that the evil could happen. The lesson of the
potter was designed for men skeptical of hope. It says:
If now God promises to rebuild the destroyed land and
to replant the uprooted people, believe him. He is able.[11]

To the exiles of 598 Jeremiah had spoken with similar
intent. What he wrote to them was comfort because they
were the uprooted, but only half-comfort because something had not yet happened. Jeremiah's letter in chapter
29 is to be understood along with his parable of figs in
chapter 24. Before the temple Jeremiah saw two baskets
of figs; "the one basket was very good figs like first-fruit
figs, and the other basket was very bad figs, too bad to
eat." And Jeremiah thought of those who had been removed from their land in 598 together with their king
Jehoiachin, and he thought of the men left in Jerusalem
and of the new king Zedekiah, and he understood the
meaning of the two baskets of figs; he knew that a good
fate was in store for the earlier exiles now on foreign soil
and he knew equally that the fate destined for them that
yet remained, behind the ramparts of Zion, was bad, very
bad. That was the word he had from God.

[11] Compare the chapter entitled "Hope is a Duty" in Blank, *Prophetic
Faith in Isaiah* (especially p. 180), on Isa. 59.

. . . Like these good figs, so I will regard for their good the exiles of Judah whom I have sent from this place to Chaldaea . . . and like the bad figs, too bad to eat, . . . I will ill [12] treat Zedekiah, the king of Judah, and his nobles and the rest of Jerusalem that are left in this land . . . and I will make them a byword for all the kingdoms of the earth . . . (24:5, 8-9).

It is not the promise but the threat that dominates the chapter. The interpretation of the basket of bad figs is the climax and the point: Zedekiah and those left in Jerusalem will follow the earlier exiles to Babylon. There is comfort in the comparison. The already uprooted have no more to fear for themselves—that is the comfort; but it is only half-comfort—their restoration awaits the stroke which is yet to descend upon their brothers in Jerusalem.

It is this message which Jeremiah conveyed to the first group of exiles—those of 598—who awaited better news. One of the prophets among them there in Babylon rightly understood what Jeremiah meant by his advice: "Build houses and live in them. Plant gardens and eat their produce" (29:5). That prophet, Shemaiah, reduced Jeremiah's message to two Hebrew words: 'arukkah hi': "It will be long" (29:28). That is what he understood Jeremiah to mean: "It will be long." "Long" is not forever, and therein lay the hope. But time enough to live in newly built houses and to enjoy the fruits of newly planted gardens is at any rate a while, and therein lay the disappointment. One who shared Shemaiah's indignation was Hananiah, a contemporary of that prophet. In Jerusalem Hananiah was saying for God: "In another two

[12] The word translated "ill" has been separated from the verb in the Hebrew text and stands in the next verse.

years I will bring back to this place all the vessels of the
Lord's house . . . and Jeconiah . . . and all the captivity of Judah" (28:3-4). To Hananiah, as to the exiles
in Babylonia, Jeremiah said it would be long—except that
to Hananiah he said it in the form of the threat that such
temple vessels as had not then been carried as trophies to
Babylonia would yet be carried off—that is to say: Jerusalem will yet be taken, the temple and palace will yet
be looted and any restoration of the former glory will
have to wait.[13]

And so it was deferred hope, hope for restoration after
a blow yet to fall, delayed comfort, that Jeremiah enclosed
in his letter to the exiles of 598.

What he said to Ephraim was long overdue. The people
of Ephraim, the northern kingdom of Israel, had suffered
exile for a full century before Jeremiah summoned to a
new hope the descendants of the originally exiled: "Come
back, Meshuvah Israel, God says, I do not frown on you;
for I am constant, God says, I bear no lasting grudge"
(3:12). "Israel" is without doubt the "lost" ten tribes;
"Meshuvah Israel" is distinguished in what precedes from
"Bagodah Judah"—to Israel's advantage. God is ready for
Israel's return—though not for Judah as yet. Here, too,
it is the already uprooted that he proposes to replant.

Jeremiah's chapters 30 and 31 are a small manual of
consolation. "Go, write what I have told you in a book"
(30:2), God said to Jeremiah, and those two chapters
are the "book." Their content is fairly uniform, and for
the most part it speaks hope for the ten tribes in distant
exile. Here in these chapters, laying aside his elegiac
mood, Jeremiah sings exultant lyrics of redemption. He
sings of Ephraim, Joseph's son, and of Rachel, mother of

[13] Jer. 27:18-22.

Joseph and symbol of the northern kingdom. Let Rachel
dry her tears:

> . . . Hark! Lamentation is heard in Ramah,
> Bitter weeping,
> Rachel weeping for her children,
> Inconsolable—[weeping] for her children
> Because they are not.
> So God said:
> Withhold your voice from weeping
> And your eyes from tears,
> For there is a reward for your labor, God says,
> And there is a hope for your latter end, God says,
> And sons will return to their borders
> And they shall return from the land of the foe (31:15-17).[14]

In dramatic dialogue God responds invitingly to Ephraim's contrition:

> I plainly heard Ephraim lamenting:
> "You disciplined me and I accepted discipline
> [Who had been] like an untrained calf.
> Now take me and let me come back,
> For you are the Lord my God.
> After I turned away I was sorry,
> And after I learned I smote my thigh.
> I knew disgrace, was indeed abashed,
> Suffered the shame of my youth."
> Is Ephraim a favorite son,
> My own dear boy,
> That as often as I speak of him
> I have to remember him again the more?
> I yearn for him;

[14] The order of the clauses of verses 16 and 17 is different in the
Hebrew.

My compassion towards him is aroused, God says.
Set up signposts;
Make yourselves way-markers.
Give thought to the road,
The way you went.
Come back, O virgin Israel;
Return here to your cities.
Why are you timid,
O wayward daughter? (31:18-22).

In two similar passages the bitter past, the day of Assyria's triumph and Samaria's fall, still distressingly present, yields to comfort, though in a few words only, at the very end of each composition:

. . . Hark! We have heard terror,
Fright without relief!
Ask and observe;
Does a male bear children?
Why have I seen every man
With hands on thighs like a woman in childbirth,
And every face turned pale?
Ah, indeed great was that day,
Incomparable!
It was a grievous time for Jacob—
But from it he will be delivered (30:5-7).

"But from it he will be delivered"—that is the climax and the whole comfort.

For so God said:
Grievous was your breaking,
Heavy the blow you suffered,
With no . . . remedy for the sore,
For you no healing.

All your friends forgot you,
They did not seek you out,
Because I struck you as an enemy strikes,
With a cruel man's discipline,
In consequence of the magnitude of your guilt,
In consequence of the multitude of your sins.
Why do you cry because of your breaking,
[Because] your pain is grievous?
It was in consequence of the magnitude of your guilt,
In consequence of the multitude of your sins
That I did these things to you . . .
[Now] indeed I will bring you healing;
I will cure you of your wounds, God says,
For they called you rejected,
[Saying:] ". . . She has none to look after her" (30:12-15,
    17).

Compared to this little in these two passages ("From it
he will be delivered" and "I will bring you healing; I
will cure you of your wounds"), the next is an unabridged
promise, endless consolation:

So God said:
I will restore the tents of Jacob
And show compassion to his dwelling places,
And a city will be built [again] on its mound,
And a tower will rise on its proper site;
And their song of thanksgiving will sound,
And the voice of the merrymakers;
And I will multiply them and they will not be few,
And I will increase them and they will not grow less;
And his sons will be as of old,
And his company will be secure in my presence;
And with all who would oppress him I will deal;
And his king will be of him,

And his ruler will come out of his midst,
And I will draw him near, and he will approach me,
. . . God says (30:18-21).

Another passage seems to look beyond the rebuilding
of Samaria in the North even to Jerusalem's eventual
restoration:

So God said:
In the wilderness it has found mercy—
The people left of the sword;
Israel has found repose,
Its [15] God has appeared from afar:
I love you with a lasting love;
Therefore I extend you [my] devotion.
I will yet build you up and you will be rebuilt,
O virgin Israel.
Yet will you take yourselves timbrels
And go in the dance of the merrymakers.
Yet will you plant vineyards in the hills of Samaria . . .
Yes, there will be a day when watchmen will proclaim,
In the hill country of Ephraim:
"Arise and let us go to Zion,
To the Lord our God" (31:2-6).

With such promise and lyrical hope Jeremiah consoled
the distant exiles from an earlier time. And this now is
to be observed: that those whom he comforts in the book-
let made up of chapters 30 and 31 resembled the others
who might hope, in one distressing particular: they too
were deprived of their former delusions. According to the
total evidence, Jeremiah proffered hope (1) to the exiles
from the northern kingdom, (2) to the exiles of 598, (3)
to the survivors of the anticipated final fall of Jerusalem

[15] Reading *lo* for *li*.

and ensuing deportation, and (4) to the survivors of all of these calamities who were prepared to flee to Egypt after Gedaliah's murder. What they all shared was the experience of insecurity, the knowledge that they were not safe—they shared their lost illusions. Because in fact or in prospect it had already happened, they would no more say it could not happen. In fact or in prospect their capital city was in ruins and they were uprooted and their God had not protected them.

In a certain sense, persons of another category may be joined with these. They are the persons who could attain the insight without the experience, who knew before walls fell that Jerusalem was vulnerable, and even before the temple was violated knew well that God and his house were not identical. Then as now there were men of quick imagination who did not need to be shown. Two of these are named in Jeremiah's book; they were Baruch the scribe and Eved-melech. God promised both of them that they should have their life for reward. To the latter he explained the boon; it was "because you trusted me, God says" (39:18).[16] The company of Rechabites, for a related cause, merited a like reward and heard the same promise. But most closely related to the listed ones—to the exiles of Ephraim, to the Judeans deported in 598, and all such bodily uprooted and undeceived—were those defenders of Jerusalem who responded to Jeremiah's appeal, if any did, and gave up the defense and surrendered to the Babylonians. Jeremiah knew Jerusalem to be unconditionally doomed and yet he offered life to such as could choose life—and that offer at that juncture was a configuration of hope.

[16] See above, pp. 55 f., and compare Jer. 45:5 and the discussion above, pp. 144-47.

It is in this context that the question of Jeremiah's
"patriotism" should be studied, and it is against this background that his activities in the last months of Jerusalem
can be understood. It is not surprising that the princes
at that time accused him to their king of "weakening the
hands of the warriors . . . and of the whole population"
and desiring "not the welfare of this people but their ruin"
(38:4).[17] He had said enough to bring suspicion on himself. A composite of quotations from the exhortation which
the princes found offensive has this appearance:

> So God has said: I am handing this city over to Babylon's
> king and he will destroy it by fire, and you yourself [Zede-
> kiah] will not escape him, but you will be caught and
> handed over to him, and your eyes will look into the eyes
> of Babylon's king, and you will speak mouth to mouth with
> him and will come to Babylon . . . So God has said: I
> offer you a way of life and a way of death: Whoever remains
> in this city will die by the sword, by famine, or by disease.
> But whoever goes and surrenders to the Chaldaeans who
> are attacking you, will live and his life will be his reward.
> For I have turned my gaze upon this city for ill and not for
> good, God says; it will be handed over to Babylon's king
> and he will destroy it by fire. If you fight the Chaldaeans
> you will not succeed (34:2-3; 21:8-10; 32:5b).[18]

He said enough to be thought a traitor, enough clearly
to call his patriotism into question. And it may seem odd
that one employs this passage to document the prophet's
hope. Yet it is peculiarly suitable. The clue to its signifi-
cance is the expression "his life will be his reward"
(21:9). This is the third time that the expression has ap-

[17] See above, p. 53.
[18] See above, pp. 52 f.

peared in passages here reviewed. It is this same hope—
nothing more than this—that Jeremiah held out to Baruch,
and that he held out to Eved-melech; also, in substance
the same though expressed in other words, it is this hope
with which he rewarded the Rechabites.[19] And to whom
did he offer the hope of survival in the last days of Jerusalem? To those defenders of the city whose imagination
served them in the stead of experience, who wanted no
demonstration because they had the imagination required
to accept in advance the fact of Jerusalem's end. It was,
to be sure, a contingent hope, depending upon a human
choice. The "way of death" was as near at hand as the
"way of life," and for all but the few the "way of death"
exercised the greater fascination. And therefore Jeremiah
leaned to despair even while he pleaded.

It is not on record that any in fact accepted his counsel
and deserted. Zedekiah's flight is not described as a surrender calculated to secure favorable treatment for his
person, and certainly neither he nor his sons received
favorable treatment at the hands of Babylon's king.[20] But
for an understanding of Jeremiah's hope the lack or presence of candidates for hope is of no great moment; the
point is this: that Jeremiah could extend his promise to
any who would share with him his knowledge that Jerusalem was vulnerable. The hypothetical few who were
prepared in advance to act upon such knowledge might
join the hopeful ranks of those who in retrospect possessed
such knowledge—a consequence of their own bitter experience.

As to the prophet's patriotism, then, there need be no
enduring suspicion. Hoping against hope that some

---

[19] Jer. 45:5; 39:18; 35:19.
[20] Jer. 52:5-11 and II Kings 25:2-7; see above, p. 44.

might respond, he offered survival by the one way which to him seemed open. He showed no lack of love for his people when he tried to rescue such as he might from the conflagration. Recklessly he put himself in personal danger, as his experience surely proved, to save that remnant. No professing patriot could have done more.

If, then, Jeremiah seems to us to have been playing into the hands of Babylonia, seems to have been an agent for the enemy, we must be mistaking his role. Furthermore, it was not as an observer of international affairs, nor as a military expert that he spoke. He was a prophet in the biblical sense, speaking for God. Jeremiah had one master only, and that was no human king. There is a matter, too, about which there should be no ambiguity: it was not Babylonia's king who was attacking Jerusalem, it was God.

The appropriate questions are not: Was Jeremiah a patriot? and Was Jeremiah working for Babylon? The questions are: Why did Jeremiah believe that Jerusalem was doomed? Why must God destroy his temple in Zion? Or, in other words, in view of the shape of Jeremiah's hope: Why must hope linger until the blow had fallen? Why was there no future save for the uprooted, no prospect except for the homeless?

XV

Perspective

The lasting import of Jeremiah's message resides in the answer to the question so rephrased. Why was it that Jeremiah saw no road to redemption that did not cross the rubble of Jerusalem's walls and the ashes of the sanctuary?

Jeremiah may not indeed have started out with the conviction that hope could only follow on the crashing of the city walls, but with it he surely ended. He may well have set out to recall an errant people and reform a corrupt society. The word "return" was often in his mouth, and also the optimistic word "perhaps," 'ulai. Initially it was for him no mission of despair. The lack of justice, the prevalence of impurity, deceit, and oppression, the proud unconcern of the rich and mighty, aroused Jeremiah to action, and with good courage he set out to right the social wrongs. He called for "knowledge of God" and identified this knowledge with justice and righteousness. He called for constancy and devotion to God, for faithfulness and a willingness to listen. But he addressed "uncircumcised hearts" and could not be heard—so that he despaired of communicating, ever. Nor was musar of any use; the means that God had employed directly, the disciplinary acts of God—those unmediated by his prophets—they too had proved ineffective. The people seemed to close their minds; it was more comfortable so. Nothing must disturb their ease.

Indeed that is why Jeremiah could see no future except after the final curtain, why he came to speak of the fall of Jerusalem, the demolition of the temple, the removal of the people from their land to another, as of the inevitable. These things had now become symbols to him. He seemed to know that one, final, radical step had to be taken. That step would serve as a dramatic demonstration, convincing now by reason of its decisive nature—necessary because nothing else availed—the demonstration that neither the ramparts of Jerusalem nor the assumed divine presence in the Jerusalem sanctuary was their safety, that the reliance of its citizens on a patron god was precarious, that God was greater than they knew.

When Jeremiah spoke of the fall of Jerusalem and exile, he did not do so as a political realist or as a general and strategist; he spoke a different language. Also he did not interpret the approaching defeat and captivity of Judah as a punishment demanded by God. These calamities were no punishment, no payment to appease an offended deity nor explosion to relieve the tension in an angry God. They were simply a symbol, a demonstration, an argument for the unlimited greatness of God. They were to be a final act of *musar*, not punitive but educational, putting matters now in their proper light, arousing a sense of proportion, creating perspective.

To depict the future, Jeremiah did not just add brighter tones to an old picture; he used a different canvas. In order to partake of the hope his people had to step out of one frame and into another. They had to leave something behind, to abandon the old before inheriting the new. They had to leave confidence behind and the comforts of an easy religion. They must accept the responsibilities of maturity. Before they could find security they must have their eyes opened. They must cast off an outgrown parochialism and go out among strangers. They had to leave home.

And as for their view of God, they had to surrender the myth that he was a local God, residing in Jerusalem and limited to his parish.

Jeremiah had these thoughts and he made them explicit. When he wrote to the exiles of 598 in Babylon he bade them seek God even there and assured them of God's response. He told them God's word to them:

> And you shall call unto me . . . and pray to me, and I will hear you. And you shall seek and find me. If you seek me with your whole heart, I will be responsive to you, God says . . . (29:12-14).

There is no geography to God.

Jeremiah also put this thought more forcibly. And when he did so he closely paralleled an earlier thought of the first Isaiah. Isaiah said:

> The bed is too short to stretch out in,
> And the coverlet is too narrow to get under (Isa. 28:20)

and he meant: deluded by a too narrow philosophy this confiding people enjoys only the illusion of security. They can not hide under those covers; those wraps will not keep them warm.

And in his day, in turn, Jeremiah heard God's questions:

> Am I a God of near-at-hand, God says,
> And not a God of far-away? . . .
> The heavens and the earth—
> Do I not fill them? God says (Jer. 23:23 f.).

And the implications of God's questions for Jeremiah are the same as the implications of Isaiah's declaration. Without vision, without perspective, a people must perish.

Jeremiah's particular has also become a universal. The private word of God to the prophet's fleeing self had quite the same import as his new word to the people. For the prophet the Jordan jungle was the world's challenge —his "far-away."

> If even in a land at peace you fall down
> How would you do in the jungle of the Jordan? (Jer. 12:5)

And now, more broadly, God asks of a people with undiminished challenge:

> The heavens and the earth—
> Do I not fill them?

Jeremiah's way was not contentment; peace of mind was not his destination.

The religion of Jeremiah sought out the more distant goals, the broader horizons. The God of Jeremiah pressed against the walls of Jerusalem and the borders of Judah; these would not confine him.

Jeremiah did not see anger in the eyes of God; he saw love—and sorrow. He did not see God casting his people

off; he saw God letting his people go, regretfully relin-
quishing his hold. God was surrendering his people; although it cost him pain he was permitting a stubbornly
heedless people to destroy itself.

Translate that thought for our day. Contemplate the
contingency that today God could part with his earth-
creature, man, that not in anger but with sorrow God could
renounce mankind. Perspective grows with the thought—
a live awareness of our peril. Is there meaning for us in
Jeremiah? His perspective, activated, could be our salvation.

Jeremiah's times and ours share a certain spirit. An
expanding spirit breathed in his day as it does in ours.
Our religion, too, is bursting from its bounds—a challenge
to the hardy mind. It summons to tasks beyond one's
mental grasp, to unaccustomed sacrifice, to risk and labor
for the distant and unknown.

Jeremiah is companion to the daring. And hope is something that you *do*.

Additional Notes

FIRST ADDITIONAL NOTE: DATES, KINGS, AND
CHAPTERS IN SECTION I
(See Chap. I, n. 1.)

Jeremiah served as prophet during the last decades of the
Judean monarchy and the first few years of the Babylonian
captivity, i.e., in the last third of the seventh pre-Christian
century and the early part of the sixth, roughly from 630 to
580 B.C.

That was the period of the decline and eclipse of Assyria.
In 612 B.C. Nineveh, the capital of Assyria, fell to the Medes
and Babylonians. In 605 B.C. at Carchemish these same two
powers conclusively defeated the Assyrians together with
their Egyptian allies. The two events marked the end of the
Assyrian empire and the beginning of Babylonian ascendancy.
While Jeremiah lived the rulers of those kingdoms "between
the rivers" included Ashurbanipal (668-626) and Ashur-uballit
(612-605), of Assyria, and Nabopolassar (625-605) and Nebuchadrezzar II (605-562), of Babylonia. (The data in this paragraph and the next are taken in part from *The Monuments and
the Old Testament* by Price, Sellers, and Carlson [Philadelphia,
1958], pp. 281-304, 413-14.)

These were the Judean kings in the life of Jeremiah: *Josiah;*
Josiah's son *Jehoahaz;* another of Josiah's sons, *Jehoiakim;*
Jehoiakim's son *Jehoiachin;* and the last reigning son of Josiah,
Zedekiah. Their dates are fairly certain:

Josiah	640-609
Jehoahaz (three months)	609
Jehoiakim	609-598
Jehoiachin (three months)	598
Zedekiah	598-587

The governor Gedaliah (587–*circa* 582) followed on the kings. The two last kings were forcibly removed from the throne and taken as captives to Babylonia, Jehoiachin with many of his people in 598, Zedekiah with others in 587. That was the year (587) in which Nebuchadrezzar took Jerusalem after a siege of nearly two years and looted and burned the temple. The opening verses of the book of Jeremiah, a sort of title page, bracket the prophet's life between Josiah and the Exile:

The words of Jeremiah . . . who had the word of God in the days of Josiah, Amon's son, king of Judah, in the thirteenth year of his reign, and in the days of Jehoiakim, Josiah's son, king of Judah, until the end of the eleven years of Zedekiah, Josiah's son, king of Judah, until Jerusalem's exile in the fifth month (1:1-3).

The title verses leave unmentioned the three-month kings, Jehoahaz and Jehoiachin, and they stop short of Gedaliah, with whom also Jeremiah was associated, but they name the three royal principals, Josiah, Jehoiakim, Zedekiah. According to the specific date, "the thirteenth year" of Josiah, Jeremiah's prophetic ministry began in the year 628 B.C. He is last heard of in Egypt several years after the fall of Jerusalem, i.e., about 580 B.C. (Jer. 44).

In Jeremiah's book the sequence of chapters is not chronological. Here, in Section I of the present work, we consider the biographical material in an order related to the order of the events in Jeremiah's life. A tabular view here follows; the figures in parentheses are dates—often only approximate:

SECTION I

Chapter I: *from the time of Jehoiakim:* Jer. 7:1-15 and
               chap. 26 (609 B.C.).

Chapter II: *from the time of Jehoiakim:* Jer. 36; 25:1-14
               and chap. 45 (606, since the "fifth" year in 36:9
               is less probable than the "fourth" in 36:1—see
               25:1 and 45:1).

Chapter III: *from the time of Jehoiakim:* Jer. 19 and 20:
               1-6 (*circa* 600) and chap. 35 (598);
               from the time of Zedekiah: Jer. 29 (*circa* 595);
               27 and 28 (594—the two chapters belong to-
               gether and the date in 28:1 is supported by
               27:3, 12 as against the misleading 27:1); 21:1-7
               and 37:17-21 (588-587).

Chapter IV: *from the time of Zedekiah:* Jer. 34:8-22 and
               37:7-10; 37:11-16; 38; 21:8-10; 34:2-3; 32:3-5;
               39:15-18; 32:6-15 (588-587);
               from the time of Gedaliah: 39:1-14; 40:1-41:3;
               after the death of Gedaliah: 41:4-44:30.

SECOND ADDITIONAL NOTE: TWO TERMS FOR PRAYER
(See pp. 95 f., text.)

The word *paga'* occurs in the sense of "intercede" only ten
times in the Bible, and more often in Jeremiah than in any
other book. Three of the passages from Jeremiah have been
quoted above: "Do not pray for this people or take up for
them any cry or prayer or intercede [*tiphga'*] with me" (7:16);
"I have interceded [*hiphga'ti*] with you . . . in the time of
calamity and the time of disaster" (15:11); "If they be prophets . . . let them intercede [*yiphge'u*] with the Lord of hosts

that the vessels . . . come not to Babylon" (27:18). The one other passage in Jeremiah is an intercession not involving God but among men. Certain persons in the court of Jehoiakim "interceded [*hiphgi'u*] with the king that he should not burn the scroll, but he did not listen to them" (36:25). There are two further biblical instances of such intercession among persons. Abraham said to the Hittites: "Intercede [*pige'u*] for me with Ephron the son of Zohar that he may give me the cave of Machpelah" (Gen. 23:8 f.); and Ruth said to Naomi, her mother-in-law: "Do not entreat [*tiphge'i*] me to leave you" (Ruth 1:16), in which latter passage the word has a slightly different meaning. But in the remaining passages intercession is with God. In one in Job the activity is simply that of entreaty, as in Ruth; the "wicked" say: "What is the Almighty, that we should serve him? And of what avail is it that we should entreat [*niphga'*] him?" (Job 21:15).

Finally, the term appears three times in the latter chapters of Isaiah, in 47:3 and 59:16, and in chapter 53, where it is used of the "servant." Here, as often, we may note the influence of Jeremiah upon the Second Isaiah; a word—this word—in a not too common meaning is found mainly in these two of the prophets—in Jeremiah and the Second Isaiah. In Isaiah 47:3 God, pictured here as the zealous defender of his enslaved people, prepared now to exact recompense from their captors, makes known his resolution: he will hear no argument. With a necessary change in the vowel points, that is the meaning of the word in this passage: "I will have revenge and not accept intercession [*'eppagea'*]." A substantive form of the verb appears in 59:16 with the sense of one who intervenes to remedy a situation. According to this later Isaiah, at a time when truth was lacking and justice failed, God

. . . saw that there was no man,
Was amazed that there was no one to intervene [*maphgia'*];

so then

> . . . his own arm wrought for him salvation,
> And his sure purpose sustained him.

(See Blank, *Prophetic Faith in Isaiah,* p. 156, for the meaning: "sure purpose.")

The one remaining passage in which the verb has this special meaning is a part of the fourth "servant song," the promise with which the song concludes. There, in 53:11 f., God says of the servant, his people—a people whose long record of service and suffering is drawing to a close:

> My servant vindicated many,
> Bearing their iniquities;
> Therefore I will give him a portion among the many,
> He shall share spoil among the mighty,
> Because he emptied his life even to death
> And was counted among transgressors
> And bore the guilt of many,
> Intervening for the transgressors.

(See Blank, *op. cit.,* pp. 88, 91, 93, 95 f.)

The word occurs in the final clause: "intervening [*yaphgia*'] for the transgressors." There is much reason to believe that the Second Isaiah used Jeremiah as his prophetic model when he drew the figure of the "servant," his personification of Israel cast in the role of a prophet-people. (Blank, *op. cit.,* pp. 100 ff.) And it is significant that he chose to mention this feature too, among those features which the servant shared with his prototype. The prophet-people Israel interceded with God on behalf of other transgressors as the prophet Jeremiah had done on behalf of his people.

Along with the verb *paga*' the Hebrew *palal* appears in Jeremiah, and frequently elsewhere. In the Bible it is in fact the usual verb for praying, and the derived noun *tephillah* is the common word for prayer (this does not need demonstration). The verb appears twice in the letter which Jeremiah wrote to his people in Babylonian exile urging them to pray to God in that land, and it appears when the prophet himself is involved in the praying. Jeremiah, speaking for God in the letter which he dispatched to the exiles, counseled them: "Seek the welfare of the city to which I have exiled you and pray [hithpallelu] for it to God, for in its welfare is your welfare." And he also said: "Call on me . . . and pray [hithpallaltem] to me, and I will hear you. Seek and you will find me" (29:7 and 12). As for his own praying the principal passages have been cited: the restraining words of God: "Pray [tithpallel] not for good for this people" (14:11), and "Do not pray [tithpallel] for this people, or take up for them any cry or prayer [tephillah], or intercede with me" (7:16, repeated in 11:14); and the request of the fugitives: "Let our petition sway you and pray [hithpallel] to the Lord your God on our behalf" (42:2, repeated in 42:20), to which, despite the divine restraint, he assented: "I have heard; I will pray [mithpallel] to the Lord your God as you say" (42:4). (Re 32:16; 37:3, see Fourth Additional Note, pp. 243 f.)

The broad meaning is clear: palal means "to pray." But there are also overtones of meaning that lend special interest to the word. These overtones derive from the use of this word in a legal context. Appearances here may be deceptive. Possibly biblical Hebrew possessed homonyms—a palal related to worship and a palal at home in the law courts. At any rate, there are a number of passages in which the verb and its derivatives have to do with judging or deciding, defending a litigant or rendering a verdict, and these overtones sound even when the word means "to pray." The text is not always above suspicion and the meaning is sometimes ambiguous (therefore the occasional question marks), but enough is clear to establish the general sense. Where "absolve," "judge," "defend," and the like, occur in the following passages the Hebrew text contains a form or a derivative of the verb palal, the verb which also means "to pray" (or a homonym of that verb).

> If a man sins against a man God can absolve [?] him [*u-philelo*], but if a man sins against God who can defend [?] him [*yithpallel lo*]? (I Sam. 2:25).

> You defended [*pillalt le-*] your sisters by reason of your sins which were more abominable than theirs [so that your sisters] seem more virtuous than you (Ezek. 16:52).

> Phineas stood and rendered judgment [*vayephallel*].
> And the plague subsided (Ps. 106:30).

> Provide counsel, render judgment [*pelilah*].
> Let your shade at noontide be like night.
> Shelter the outcasts; do not leave a fugitive unprotected (Isa. 16:3).

> Their rock is not like our Rock
> Even if our enemies serve as judges [*pelilim*]
>   [i.e., even in their estimation] (Deut. 32:31).

> . . . He shall be fined the amount that the woman's husband shall fix and he shall give it with judges [arbitrating ?, *biphelilim*] (Exod. 21:22).

> [Prophets] reel when acting as seer;
> [Priests] totter in the act of judgment [? *peliliyah*]
>   (Isa. 28:7).

> That would be a transgression to be condemned [i.e., judged wrong, *pelili*],
> For I would have deceived God on high (Job 31:28, v. 11 similar).

If these passages are here correctly interpreted, and if this legal element in the root is thus established, with judging, estimating, defending, acquitting, as phases of the basic meaning, the prayers in the Bible may, if not always then sometimes, be a pleading, may partake of the nature of a defendant's plea in a court of law, his representations before his judge. *Tephillah* may have overtones of argument, plea, defense. There is, indeed, one passage in which no interpretation of the word suits the context so well as this. It is in Psalm 109. The psalmist is surrounded by enemies who would requite him evil for good (v. 5). He curses them. He would have such a one brought to trial with an accuser beside him; he would see the adversary judged guilty, his defense serving only to convict him. He says of his opponent:

When he is judged let him go forth the loser;
Let his plea establish his guilt (Ps. 109:7).

The word here translated "plea" is the common biblical word for prayer, *tephillah*. In this passage, at least, there sound loud and clear the overtones of plea and defense.

This latter is the element which is dominant in Jeremiah's prayers on his own behalf. (See Chapter VIII; see also my footnote 12 in *Hebrew Union College Annual*, XXI, 337 f.)

THIRD ADDITIONAL NOTE: "AMEN"
(See p. 97, text.)

The word "amen" seems to have been at home in a ceremony in the course of which a man (or even a tribe or a city) makes a binding promise, conditionally accepts for himself the terms of a curse, becomes liable if he has sworn falsely. The one administering the oath (priest, judge, Levites, or whoever) puts the conditional curse in the form of a statement, to which the one taking the oath responds with an "amen" which in this context means as much as "right, so it is, or so be it; I accept; if I be false let the curse be fulfilled in me." With his "Amen" he makes himself liable.

The ordeal of a woman suspected of adultery is an example:

And the priest shall cause her to swear, and shall say unto the woman: ". . . if thou be defiled, and some man have lain with thee besides thy husband . . . this water that causeth the curse shall go into thy bowels, and make thy belly to swell, and thy thigh to fall away"; and the woman shall say: "Amen, Amen" (Num. 5:19-22, JPS translation).

"Amen" is her assent; it is as though she herself said the words that made her liable.

It is the same with the twelvefold "Amen" spoken by the men of Israel assembled at Gerizim and Ebal, in Deut. 27:14-26. After each of twelve curses the people thus respond and their response means: "So be it, let me indeed be cursed if I become guilty of this offense." The introduction to this ceremony and an example here follow:

And the Levites shall speak, and say unto all the men of Israel with a loud voice:
". . . Cursed be he that removeth his neighbor's landmark." And all the people shall say: "Amen" (vv. 14, 17, JPS).

In time the primitive oath form was replaced by one in which God was involved, and men said: "Thus may God do to me and even more [if I do, or do not do, so and so]." Eli employed this formula when he adjured the young Samuel to tell him all that God had disclosed to him: "God do so to thee, and more also, if thou hide anything from me . . ." (I Sam. 3:17, JPS). The proper response on Samuel's part, though not recorded, was an "Amen, so may God do," just as in Jeremiah's exclamatory prayer when Hananiah had finished: "Amen! So may God do! Let God but fulfill the words of your prophecy . . ." (28:6).

The confirmatory "Amen" may have stood along with an oath in another passage in Jeremiah. In 15:11 we should probably restore *'amen* (with the Greek translation) where now the Hebrew text reads *'amar.* Here the word would mean something like "Indeed!"—"Indeed, Lord!" Two affirmations introduced by the words *'im lo'*, words which normally introduce affirmatory oaths, follow the exclamation "Amen!" in 15:11. Twice, then, Jeremiah used the term in preserved utterances: in 15:11 and in 28:6, the encounter with Hananiah. (The "Amen, Lord!" in 11:5, used as in 15:11, stands in a passage wrongly attributed to Jeremiah; see Fourth Additional Note, below.)

FOURTH ADDITIONAL NOTE: OMISSIONS
(See Chap. IV, n. 16; Chap. V, nn. 8, 9; Chap. VII, n. 7; Chap. XIV, n. 5 *et passim.*)

Parts of the book of Jeremiah are advisedly omitted from the foregoing study. The most obvious omission is that block of chapters (46-51—with 43:8-13 and 44:30) which concern peoples other than Israel. The six chapters are to be classified with groups of similar compositions in Ezekiel (chaps. 25-32, 35) and Isaiah (chaps. 13-16, 19, 21, 23), and it is customary to refer to these and related chapters collectively (and inaccurately) as "oracles against the nations." They constitute a genre apart, and whether or not any of them can be related to events dating from Jeremiah's lifetime, they are not especially relevant in a study of his prophetic personality. They are arbitrarily omitted from this study—and with them certain similar material, e.g., 25:15-38.

Significantly, in the Greek translation of Jeremiah this second half of Jer. 25 is grouped with the six chapters 46 to 51. Moreover, these six chapters appear in the Greek in a different place. Otherwise arranged also, chapters 46 to 51 are inserted between the two parts of chapter 25. Possibly these "oracles against the nations," together with the latter part of chapter 25, were once a separate collection of such utterances with no fixed order, which collection was in time incorporated into Jeremiah's book; but in the ancestor of our Hebrew text, in one place, and in the copy which the Greek translator used, in another.

Along with this bulkier material an editor probably added a few phrases to make more plausible the presence of these chapters, phrases like "and against all these nations round about," in 25:9; "against all the nations," in 25:13; "and against all the nations," in 36:2; and the words "to the nations" and "to the nations and to the kingdoms" in the prophet's consecration vision in sentences which now read: "Before you went from the womb I adopted you; I designated you a prophet *to the nations*" (1:5) and "See, I have designated you today [a prophet] *to the nations and to the kingdoms*" (1:10).

In addition to this one collection of material concerned with foreign peoples, certain other less extensive intrusions now appear within the book of Jeremiah. For example, the greater part of 39:1-14 and chapter 52 appear again as II Kings 24:18-25:30 and this matter seems (like Isa. 36-39) originally to have been at home in Kings instead of in Jeremiah (or Isaiah). The narrative of Jeremiah's treatment at the hands of Nebuzaradan in 40:1-6 parallels the historical kernel of 39:1-14, but it contains additional legendary features that cast doubt on its originality, e.g., the reported words of the Babylonian commander to Jeremiah: "The Lord your God announced that this calamity would befall this place, and he brought it on and did as he had spoken" (40:2b-3a)—words natural in the mouth of a Jeremiah or a Zechariah (see Zech. 1:6), but hardly to be expected from this Chaldaean warrior. They are a step in the direction of the rabbinic legend which told that Nebuzaradan became a convert to Judaism (*Talmud Babli*, Giṭṭin, 57b; cf. *Hebrew Union College Annual*, XII-XIII, 338 f.). Again, the narrative of Zedekiah's interview with Jeremiah in 38:14-27 parallels the narrative of the second interview in 37:17-21, and the version in chapter 38 may well be a later legendary account of that same incident and not the record of a third such encounter. Jeremiah is much more "in character" in 37:17-21 than in 38:14-27 (cf. Buttenwieser, *Prophets of Israel*, pp. 56-62).

The book of Jeremiah also includes compositions which so nearly approximate in style and, more significantly, in thought, the expressions of other biblical writers, that they must be regarded as additions made under the influence of these others. The thought of the Second Isaiah so dominates such passages as Jer. 10:1-16 and 31:7-13, for example, that these could hardly have been composed before his time. The exhortation to Sabbath observance in 17:19-27 is so little in the spirit of Jeremiah as he appears elsewhere, and so much more congenial to such a one as Nehemiah (see Neh. 13:15-22) or the author of Isa. 56, that it may well be a product of the fifth century. The language in 9:11-13; 11:6-8; 16:10-13 is the language of the hortatory frame of Deuteronomy and these passages and frequent phrases besides give plausibility to the theory that the book of Jeremiah experienced a deuteronomic redaction. A passage like Jer. 11:1-13, in fact, gives rise to the suspicion that a deuteronomist added it expressly to make of Jeremiah a propagandist for the program of Deuteronomy. (For an analysis of Jeremiah's position, see above, pp. 189-92.) It may have been a deuteronomic editor who composed Jer. 37:1-7a to patch up the disorder created when 37:7b-10 was separated from 34:8-22 (see above, p. 46); at any rate, 37:1 f. are the work of a deuteronomic historian. Eschatological matter, like 23:5 and the greater part of chapter 33, has so little in common with the rest of Jeremiah and so much in common with the thought of the early post-Exilic period that it is surely intru-

sive. Jer. 32:16-44, which reads like an appendix to the earlier
part of the chapter, since what it says has there been said
already, includes a prayer (vv. 17-23) in the manner of the
early synagogue (see Ezr. 9; Neh. 9; Dan. 9).

The intention of this Additional Note is to explain, with
a limited number of examples, the omission of parts of the
book of Jeremiah in this study of the prophet Jeremiah. It
is not to suggest that the omitted matter is inferior in thought
or in literary power. One of the finest prayers in the Bible
is an addition to Jer. 14. It is contained in verses 7-9 and
19-22, and it is probably a prayer for rain:

> If our sins bear witness against us,
> O Lord, act for the sake of your name.
> For our lapses are many;
> Against you we have sinned.
> Hope of Israel,
> Its savior in time of distress!
> Why are you as a stranger in the land,
> As a wayfarer who has [only] turned in to lodge?
> Why are you as one amazed,
> As a warrior who can not help?
> And you are in our midst, O Lord,
> And we are called by your name.
> Do not leave us! . . .
> Have you wholly rejected Judah?
> Do you deeply loathe Zion?
> Why have you stricken us so that there is no remedy?
> Why do we hope for peace and there is no good,
> And for a time of healing and lo, terror?
> We are aware of our wickedness, O Lord,
> The guilt of our fathers, for we have sinned against you.
> For your name's sake do not spurn [us];
> Do not disdain your throne of glory.
> Remember, do not denounce your covenant with us.
> Are there among the vanities of nations those that give rain?

Or do the heavens produce showers?
Is it not you, O Lord, our God?
And for you we hope,
For you made all of these.

The prayer is no less moving if a spirit other than Jeremiah composed it.

Index of
Biblical Passages

(n = note)

General Index

Index and Glossary
of Hebrew Terms

(Listed according to the order of the Hebrew alphabet)

'ulai (perhaps), 25 f., 183, 227

'amen (may it be so), 97, 110n9, 239-241

'emunah (faithfulness), 175n1

'ari'el (altar hearth [?], Isaiah's ominous name for Jerusalem), 35

'arukkah hi' (it will be long), 217

bagodah (perfidious — Jeremiah's abusive name for Israel), 189, 218

goy (a nation), 203

da'at (knowledge), 184

hallelujah (praise the Lord), 97

hesed (commitment), 153

hasid (constant), 153

YHWH (Lord), 112

yerivai (my adversaries), 119

yarshi'eni (prove me in the wrong), 120

laken (therefore), 120, 133, 138

magor missaviv (horror round about), 36

musar (discipline), 176, 196-199, 205, 209, 227 f.

mazdiki (he who vindicates me), 120

meshugga' (madman), 37, 164

meshuvah (backslider—Jeremiah's abusive name for Judah), 218

mishpatim (cases at law), 119

nishhat (spoiled), 215

'am (a people), 203

'amal (toil), 144n2

'azur (in hiding), 27, 29 f.

paga' (pray, intercede), 96 f., 102, 234-236

pahadu (they were terrified), 29 f.

palal (pray, plead), 96 f., 236-239

zedek (sure purpose), 153n10

kal wahomer (an argument *a minori ad majus*), 144

riv (cause), 119

rodephai (they that persecute me), 119

resha'im (guilty men), 119

shuvu . . . u-shevu (return . . . and abide), 26, 31

shalom (peace), 206

shophet zedek (righteous judge), 119

tohu (chaos), 150

tehinnah (supplication), 103

tephillah (prayer as plea), 105, 121, 236-239

torah (instruction), 190